MW01001291

"I learnt that *MahaVastu*™ is a actually a scientific tool — the framework which helped me understand why things happen the way they do. The Bar Chart Technique is marvellous. It has made us identify the cut and extended portions in our house and precisely locate the problematic areas. The *MahaVastu*™ Procedure Flow Chart leaves no scope for Hit and Miss."

—Harish, *IT Professional, Delhi*

"Earlier I had so many misconceptions about *Vastu* that I could not believe in this knowledge. But I am really surprised with the logical concepts, lucidly explained in this course; how accurately they explain the reasons for various problems in life. Now, I want to give *MahaVastu*™ a sincere try in my own life".

—Dr. Seema, *MBBS, Delhi*

"I got to read *MahaVastu*™ and I found it scientifically connected, practical and logical. The course is excellent; I am very happy having done this."

—Parul Waeerkar, *M.Sc., Child Development; Graphologist; Mumbai*

ESTD 1936
AMRIT BOOK CO.
Books on History, Politics, Philosophy, Religion,
Yoga, Ayurveda, Travel, Music, Dance, Astrology,
Palmistry, Children Books, Computer, Law Management,
Medical, Civil Engineering & Hindi Books
N-21, Connaught Circus, Opp. Scindia House, New Delhi-110001
Mob.: 9810778775, 9811113613

VASTUSHASTRI KHUSHDEEP BANSAL

MahaVastu™

Om Books International

Reprinted in 2022 by
Om Books International

Corporate & Editorial Office
A 12, Sector 64, Noida 201 301
Uttar Pradesh, India
Phone: +91 120 477 4100
Email: editorial@ombooks.com
Website: www.ombooksinternational.com

Sales Office
107, Ansari Road, Darya Ganj, New Delhi 110 002, India
Phone: +91 11 4000 9000, 2326 3363, 2326 5303
Fax: +91 11 2327 8091
Email: sales@ombooks.com
Website: www.ombooks.com

Architectural Drawings: Architect Manish Kainth
Compiler: Nitin Gupta

ISBN: 978-93-80069-37-1

10 9 8 7 6 5

Printed in India

प्रार्थनामन्त्र

(Prayer *Mantra*)

वास्तुपुरुष नमस्तेऽस्तु भूशय्याभिरत प्रभो।

मद्गृहे धनधान्यादि समृद्धिं कुरु सर्वदा।।

(O Absolute Conscious Lord Of The Building,
Having Earth As Your Seat Of Creation,
I Bow To You From My Soul,
May You Always Fill
My Home With Money,
Food And Prosperity.)

LOVE AND THANKS

Manu and Amit for being a part of my being;

Architect Manish for translating my imagination into magical space;

Nitin and Vipin for their painstaking efforts in compiling
this concept;

Rachna and Vipul for making it divine with their designs;

My wonderful friends Sanjay and Ajay Mago of Om Books
International for publishing this book and turning my dream
into reality;

Shivjeet Kullar for his guidance;

Dr Rajiv-Dr Meenakshi, Harish-Mamta and *MahaVastu*™ core group
for being absorbing listeners, giving power to my thoughts.

My Di, Sunita Pant Bansal for crafting this beautiful piece of art,
through her amazing skill with words that create the world which we
live in;

Simran Anand and Sonia Bhagat for using their magical (pen) chisel to
give cut and clarity to each word;

Worshipful Masters for making me what I am;

My parents for my incarnation;

And

My son Chaitanya and daughters Ira and Princi Khushi for making me
realise what life is and wife Seema for what it is not.

FOREWORD

I have been dabbling with cosmic sciences for more than two decades now and have read a fair number of books on *Vastu*. All the books touch this subject in a manner that leaves a number of questions unanswered. Remedies done based on these books hardly give consistent results. Why? The reason is that they do not delve deeply enough into the science of *Vastu*. If they had done so, there would not have been room for any errors, as all sciences are always accurate. Science is all about accuracy. You derive a formula, repeat it any number of times and you get the same results.

Khushdeep has gone right into the inception of the science of *Vastu;* bringing out pearls of wisdom for the readers, who are interested in understanding what is going around them and why it is so and what should they do to change it...

MahaVastu™ is the real *Vastu,* as taught in the original Hindu scriptures. It has been simplified into a step-by-step self-help programme, by the author. He has derived the formula to accurately evaluate our surrounding Space, so that we are able to implement the solutions effectively. Khushdeep has left no scope for any errors in his method, as like a true scientist, he has tried and tested it thousands of times.

'We are what we think' is a well-known adage and explained beautifully by Khushdeep in the chapter on *Panchkosha*. It is inspiring to learn that we can actually 'think' ourselves to be what we want!

Who does not want bliss? It is the pursuit of every human being. After all, since we are created out of *Ananda,* we would like to return to it ... go back home, so to speak. This is the quest for *Ananda* or bliss, of every human. Once you understand the simple explanation put forward by Khushdeep, you will also understand your own restlessness and the restlessness of your soul. This itself gives you peace and inspires you to look around and find the path that is meant for your success and happiness.

And, once you understand the principle of the five elements making up the entire Universe, including us, then it will be easy to understand the havoc caused by the imbalance of those elements in your life—and how simple it is to set that right!

MahaVastu™ evaluates your Space and makes you see the imbalances, which can be easily coordinated with your real-life situation. Then it helps to set things right by the use of simple things like colours, shapes and metals. It cannot get any simpler than that!

When Khushdeep visited my office, he just shifted my workstation from one wall to another, asked my assistant to remove the red-coloured books and files from a certain wall – and hey presto! Two days later, an old client of mine gave me a great offer, doubling his earlier rate!

In another such magical instance, Khushdeep visited my brother, who has been living happily with his family in his own flat, for many years now. My brother's wife expressed a desire of acquiring more property. Khushdeep suggested putting a certain painting on a certain wall … and, unbelievably, in a couple of weeks, my brother was actually thinking, exploring and finally investing in another flat!

MahaVastu™ teaches you to reach out and realise your dreams and desires. It is simply the science of handling your Space well, which enables you to handle your life well—rightly called the 'Science of Life'.

This book, though small in size, is packed with dynamite! It has all the basic knowledge that one needs to lead a smooth, healthy, comfortable, prosperous and happy life.

Happy reading!

Sunita Pant Bansal
New Delhi, India
2010

CONTENTS

1. MahaVastu™

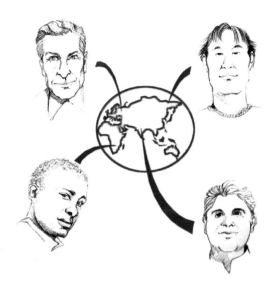

The world is full of diversity — we hear this quite often. But have you ever thought of the underlying reason behind it? Why people belonging to a particular region have similar behavioural and thought patterns?

How is it that just by looking at a person's face, you are able to tell his regional background — differentiating a South Indian from an African or an African from a Southeast Asian. Does that mean the geographical features of a region such as its land, rivers, slopes, mountains, have an influence on the lives of the people inhabiting it?

You must have noticed many a times, you enter a shop and a certain product catches your attention instantly. You end up purchasing that particular product even though you had never planned to buy it. In fact, soon after, you wonder why you bought it, when you did not need it in the first place!

On the other hand, sometimes you enter a shop with the intention of buying a certain product. You even find it, but come out of the shop not buying it. Later, you wonder why you did not purchase the product, even though it matched your choice completely!

Similarly, many homes, although beautifully designed and fastidiously maintained, make you feel oppressed, negative, unwell or just generally uncomfortable, while some which are simple, architecturally plain and common, make you feel uplifted and joyful. More importantly, they make you feel at peace with yourself and comfortable in your surroundings. The primary reason why you experience different feelings in different spaces (buildings) is their adherence to or violation of certain laws of nature. This phenomenon has been summed up as *Vastu Shastra*.

There is a continuous flow of different kinds of energies in the Universe. These energies also flow through your living space, which is in fact a scaled-down replica of the Universe itself. All aspects of your life — health, business, personal relationships, relationship with self, social networking, social reputation, fun and vigour — everything is controlled by these energies. However, the exact influence of these energies on your life is determined by the direction from which these are flowing into your space, namely, the space you inhabit. This space may be your home, office, shop, factory, and so on.

When you perform an activity in the *Vastu* zone, which is believed to be conducive for that particular activity, you attain astoundingly successful results. However, when you perform the same activity in the wrong *Vastu* zone, your results turn fruitless, sometimes even adverse. Moreover, due to the wrong activity, the inherent strength of that particular *Vastu* zone also gets weakened.

MahaVastu™ is both an art and a science that can help you achieve a balance between the activities you perform and the energies that flow through your space, in turn helping you reach your goals effectively. What *Ayurveda* is for body and *Yoga* is for mind, *MahaVastu*™ is for life!

The life which you are living now — the situations you face and the way you respond to them, the kind of people you meet, and the person that you are right now — your thoughts, emotions, creativity, confidence, skills, desires, relationships are nothing but a physical reality of the space which you inhabit. Each and every object in your space — the television, the washing machine, the flower vase, the cupboard, the mirror, the paintings, the colours — and every single space that you inhabit — the kitchen, the dining room, the toilet, the storeroom, the bedroom, the *puja* room and so on — has an impact on your subconscious mind. As you go about your daily life, your subconscious mind, like a sponge, goes on absorbing information from the objects and the activities it sees in the space around you. Accordingly, this information shapes your life.

MahaVastu™ believes that your own true self is a manifestation of the space you inhabit, namely, your home. This is the reason why, when you come back home, you take off the social masks that you wear in the world outside. Sage Patanjali has described this concept as *Swaroopen Awasthanam,* which means 'being established in your own true self'. From your home, you expect fulfillment of desires. You expect love, mental peace, relaxation, energy, success, fame, luxury, support, a better future for your children, prosperity, joy and so on. If these expectations are not met, you do not feel 'at home' and wish to run away! But where can you run? In search of a new abode, a new place to fulfil desires! A person who desperately tries to build his/her home, in truth seeks to fulfil all his/her dreams.

In what way can you attain this fulfillment? What is it that stops your dreams from being realised? *MahaVastu*™ is the science which will help you seek answers to these questions. Thus, the aim of *MahaVastu*™ is to achieve the purpose for which a building is made. For example: a school is built to educate children so that they grow into responsible adults, a hospital is built to restore people's health, and so on.

2. The Four Pillars of *MahaVastu*™

MahaVastu™ is a thoroughly systematic, logical, rational and scientific approach to *Vastu*. It is simply the ancient, time-tested wisdom of our sages, cleansed of the cobwebs of confusion that had enveloped it over thousands of years. These cobwebs appeared due to its practitioners' unwillingness to experiment and test its principles.

The contemporary version of their wisdom, namely, *MahaVastu*™, rests on the following four pillars:

  a) The *Panchtattva*
  b) The Effects of the 32 Entrances
  c) The Different Powers of the 16 *MahaVastu*™ Zones
  d) The Symbols and *Panchkosha*s

On the basis of these four pillars, *Vastushastri* Khushdeep Bansal has devised a four-step method termed as *MahaVastu*™. This method helps you evaluate your own space in order to locate the root cause of your problems. Thus, it is an aid to manifest your dream life, in which you can achieve your targets and fulfil your desires. By applying *MahaVastu*™, the purpose of your building is easily achieved and your purpose of being here on earth is fulfilled. These four pillars make *MahaVastu*™ the most reliable, scientific and unique system of *Vastu* analysis and management, with an accuracy of over 90 per cent — the highest in the world.

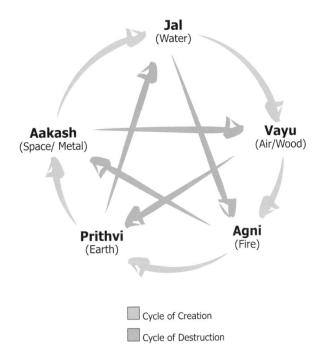

Jal
(Water)

Vayu
(Air/Wood)

Aakash
(Space/ Metal)

Agni
(Fire)

Prithvi
(Earth)

Cycle of Creation

Cycle of Destruction

Panchtattva — The Chemistry of Life

The foundation of *MahaVastu*™ is *Samkhya Yoga* (Indian Metaphysics), which is the basis of all Indian sciences like *Yoga, Ayurveda, Tantra* and many more. According to *Samkhya Yoga,* the evolution of the Universe begins with a concentrated form of pure consciousness *(Param Shiv)* and the energy of bliss *(Shakti).* This *Shiv-Shakti* union is complete and whole in itself. It is the unmanifested form of the Universe.

The Universe evolves in the form of 'five elements' from the birth-less, form-less Supreme Existence. These five elements are: *Jal, Vayu, Agni, Prithvi* and *Aakash.*

The entire Universe, whether it is the stars, the planets, the moons, or any form of life, is made up of these five elements only. Even buildings are a manifestation of these five elements, though their proportion may vary from one building to another. Each direction is dominated by one element. It is the elements which create and control the life of a building's inhabitants — the balanced state being the cause of positive, and the imbalanced state, the cause of negative effects on one's life.

In Indian metaphysics, the attributes of the five elements have been considered as *Tridosha (Vaat, Pitta* and *Kapha)* in *Ayurveda* and *Triguna (Rajas, Tamas* and *Sattva)* in *Yoga.*

In *MahaVastu*™, *Tantra* and Chinese medicine, the concept of the five elements is used in the same form as these are visible in the manifested world. Let us explore the nature, effects and properties of the five elements: *Jal, Vayu, Agni, Prithvi* and *Aakash.*

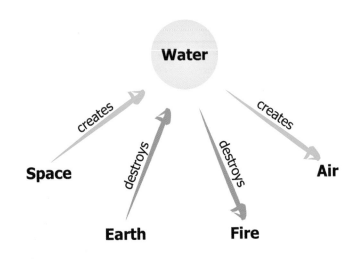

Water

Nature

It is the nature of water to flow and move on and it possesses cleansing abilities. It represents clarity, flow, generation and continuity. Accordingly, it is associated with the conception of new ideas, clarity of thought, creation of new things and vision, flow of new opportunities in life, healing energy, immunity and restoration of health. Water element dominates the North direction in buildings.

Balanced State

When Water is in a balanced state in a building, the people inhabiting it are able to see the larger picture of life. Though their attitude towards life becomes spiritual and philosophical, they are, at the core, worldly beings. They have better immunity than others and are able to cope well with life's situations. Such people create great opportunities for themselves.

Imbalanced State

When Water is in an imbalanced state in a building, it causes a nagging sense of insecurity in its occupants. Opportunities do not come their way easily and they suffer from a myopic vision of life, which is dominated by survival instincts rather than a desire to grow in life. As a result, there is no growth in their career. They are always bogged down by the burden of petty problems. Their mental peace is disturbed by trivial worries. Once things start moving out of control, it becomes difficult to restore the situation back to normalcy. Immunity gets weak leading to regular health problems.

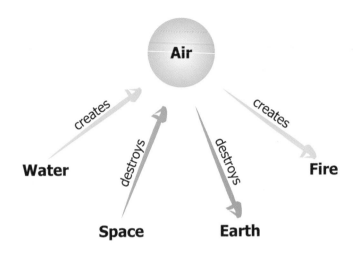

Air

Nature

The word 'air' is commonly used for vital oxygen which is provided by the plants and trees — representing growth in life. The Air element is also associated with movement, especially rotational movement. Thus, it brings refreshment, fun, joy and happiness in life. It shapes the associations you make and your position in the society. The Air element is the energy that inspires you and helps you to inspire others. It dominates the East direction and Chinese call it the Wood element.

Balanced State

In a balanced state, Air gives you the courage to try new things, take the right risks for your growth and explore your inner-self. You meet people who pave way for your growth and you perform impressively.

Imbalanced State

If not properly balanced, Air causes in an individual, stubbornness, excessive and prolonged anger, problems with neighbours or society and a feeling of being stuck. If you feel you are not able to move forward in life and petty things constantly hold you back, it's an outcome of an imbalance of the Air element in your life. In terms of health, an imbalance of the Air element leads to skin infections, joint pains and in certain cases, sexual dissatisfaction which gives way to a depressed state of mind.

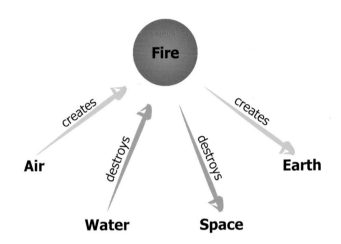

Fire

Nature

Right from the early times, Fire has been used for protection. It represents the spark, the zeal and the passion in life. Fire is the driving force behind all life processes, and thus, it is equated with money in the modern context. This element can transform your life with confidence and enthusiasm. South is the direction of Fire.

Balanced State

In its balanced state, Fire brings you fame and recognition among the masses. It gives you the zeal, power, strength, confidence and money, which become the driving force behind life and its processes. You are able to enjoy sound sleep and warmth in your relationships.

Imbalanced State

An imbalance of the Fire element in a building denies its occupants the recognition duly deserved by them. They remain unappreciated. Extreme imbalance may even bring disrepute and ill-fame, cause accidents, miscarriages, thefts and mishaps. It drains away the zeal, enthusiasm and confidence of an individual, who then tends to become introvert and fearful in nature. People living with such an imbalance face financial problems and obstacles in auspicious events — for example a marriage or a business deal. In certain cases, they face frequent health problems like acidity and indigestion.

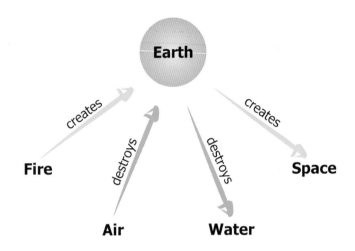

Earth

Nature

Mother Earth gives you whatever you possess and aspire for in life. Stability, balance, tenacity, solidity, rigidity, infinite patience and maturity are imbued by this element. The germination of seeds is governed by the Earth element. It provides you with the capacity to give, and it governs the process of removal of wastes from the body, thoughts, relations and life. Earth dominates the Centre and the diagonal directions of every built-up space.

Balanced State

When balanced, this element induces stability in your life — be it your career, behaviour, relationships or results of general efforts. It induces peace and harmony that you maintain with the entire world, especially with your family.

Imbalanced State

When Earth is imbalanced, it causes laziness, acute lethargy and a feeling that all your energy is drained out. Those in the service sector face job insecurity; those waiting to get married find it hard to get a suitable match. Disputes and feuds become common within the family and wasteful expenditure increases. To sum it up, imbalance of the Earth element leads to instability in relations, career and life as a whole.

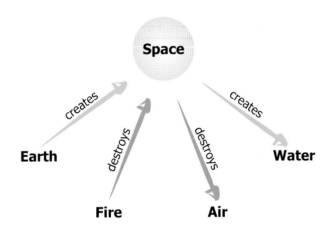

Space

Nature

Space in *Vastu* refers to something which has defined boundaries. It offers a medium for connectivity. It represents expansion, enhancement, extension, spread, communication and thought processes (mental space). Creation of new ideas, emotions, development of knowledge, relationships, blissful married life, increase in happiness, enhancement of information, business, system, support, strength (physical, emotional and financial), and the overall gain in life — are governed by the Space element. Space dominates the West direction. The Chinese call it the Metal element due to its similarity with the perfect space configuration present in metals (in their atomic structure).

Balanced State

In a balanced state, Space gives you the charge of your own destiny. It gives you a sense of direction and the ability to be organised, ensuring that you excel in everything that you do. Such a person has the ability of detached and objective introspection, and is willing to learn from past mistakes. Space gives you the knowledge and awareness to understand old beliefs and adopt new creative ideas. You are able to sharpen your skills, save more and enjoy the expected returns of your efforts.

Imbalanced State

In an imbalanced state, Space clouds wisdom. If you think you have lost your skills or that you are not getting the due returns for efforts, being unable to bring about a progressive change in things, ideas and situations, constantly feeling stuck and unclear about what to do — bring your Space back into a state of balance and harmony.

ELEMENT	COLOUR	SHAPE	
WATER	Blue	Wavy	≈
AIR	Green	Rectangular	
FIRE	Red	Triangular	▲
EARTH	Yellow	Square	
SPACE	White	Circular	○

It is the balance or imbalance among these *Panchtattva* that turns a space into virtual heaven or hell for its inhabitants. Each of these Five elements has certain attributes in the form of colours, shapes and metals. By using the attributes of the elements appropriately, the *Vastu* defects in a Space can be corrected. *Mahavastu*™ remedies offer an easy way for rectifying *Vastu* defects without resorting to actual alterations in the building structure.

To conclude, the Water element governs the North direction in every building. Air, Fire, Earth and Space govern the East, the South, the Centre and the West directions respectively. Whenever there is an imbalance, it is due to the presence of the wrong element in the wrong direction.

For example, placing the Water element (in the form of an underground water tank, water boring, blue shade or wavy shapes) in the South direction, weakens the Fire element — as Water destroys Fire *(refer to Figure on page 20).* The weakening of the Fire element will disturb the attributes of the zones (we will explain this later under the subject The 16 *MahaVastu*™ zones). Thus, placing an underground water tank in the South zone will turn a cause of anxiety, fire-accidents, restlessness and disturbed sleep. Similarly, placing the Fire element in the North zone (the zone of Water) will block new opportunities, receipt of payments, create lack of orders, these being the attributes of this zone *(refer to Figure on page 50)*. With these examples, you can see how an imbalance of the elements creates problematic situations in real life.

MahaVastu™ techniques emphasise matching the symptoms in real-life situations with the wrongly placed elements in the form of colours, shapes or physical objects in your space. Once you have identified the symptoms and matched them, be assured that the right solutions will come to you. This is the most scientific and logical approach, which will highlight the root cause of your problems and give correct solution, yielding positive results in four to six weeks, sometimes even in lesser time.

The Effects of the 32 Entrances

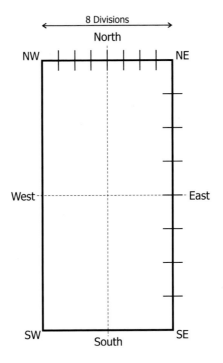

Incorrect Method

The direction which the main entrance of a building is facing, plays a very important role in the lives of its inhabitants — be it a rented accommodation or one's own property.

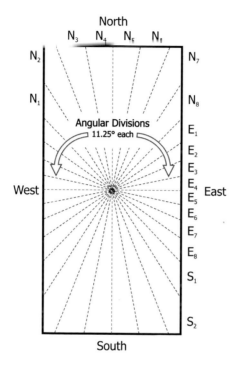

Correct Method

The location of the entrance has an independent effect on its inhabitants, which also influences the overall effect of the built-up space. The space enclosed in a building is a part of the vast space of the Universe. These two spaces represent different levels of consciousness. The space outside of a building refers to the conscious mind and the space inside represents the subconscious. Through the entrance of a space, namely, the building, one moves from one level of consciousness to another. Thus, the main door represents the shift from the conscious to the subconscious level. Also, the entrance of a building is the point at which the space enclosed by the building communicates with the Universe. Naturally, the location of a building's main entrance is very important.

Here is a common mistake made by people incorrectly using *Vastu* to determine the right location of their entrance. They divide the wall-length into eight to nine equal parts — each forming an entrance. By doing so, they sometimes come up with figures that cannot be practically implemented as dimensions. This mistake usually happens when the length-breadth ratio of the space is too large.

For example: Consider a plot (or any built-up space) of size: 60 feet (length) x 15 feet (breadth). Now, if you were to plan an entrance door along the 15 feet breadth, then, according to the commonly followed system (mentioned in *Vishwakarma Prakash*, but widely misinterpreted), we will have to divide it into 8 parts, namely, 15/8. This gives you a door-width of less than 2 feet which obviously is an impractical proposition and cannot be put into effect.

MahaVastu™ **Entrance Locations**

According to *MahaVastu*™, you determine the location of the entrance by dividing the 360° space around the Centre into 32 equal 'angular divisions'— each measuring 11.25°. By doing so, you get 32 possible locations for the entrance to your built-up space. It is this path-breaking approach of *MahaVastu*™ that places it above all other methods used in the name of *Vastu*.

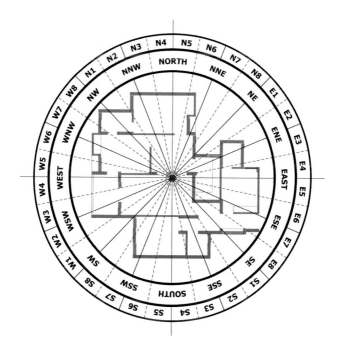

Floor Plan Divided into 32 Angular Divisions

Once you have calculated the entrance locations as per *MahaVastu*™ method, you can then match the 'symptoms of the building' with their corresponding effects. The 'symptoms of the building' refer to the good or bad situations experienced by its inhabitants. For example, some may be experiencing good things like abundance of money or success at work-place while others may be battling with negative things like delayed payments, frequent accidents, mishaps, miscarriages and so on.

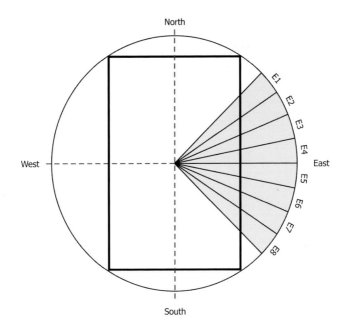

**Possible Entrance Locations in
the Eastern Segment of a Rectangular Plot**

E1 — This entrance causes fire accidents and unexpected losses.

E2 — This entrance induces wasteful expenditure. For an expecting mother, it will increase the probability of birth of baby girls.

E3 — This is an auspicious zone entrance which brings money, profits and overall success.

E4 — This entrance helps the inhabitants build beneficial and close associations with government officials or with those in authority.

E5 — This entrance makes people extremely short-tempered, bordering on insanity at times.

E6 — This entrance makes it difficult for people to keep their word, making them appear unreliable.

E7 — People in such houses become insensitive towards the problems of other people.

E8 — This entrance paves way for accidents, financial losses, burglary and other such problems.

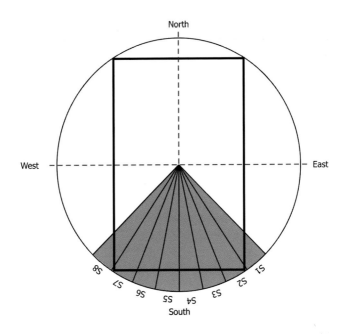

**Possible Entrance Locations in
the Southern Segment of a Rectangular Plot**

S1 — This entrance negatively impacts children, especially the boys of the house. Their actions go against their parents' expectations.

S2 — This entrance increases the tendency to work for others. It is good for people working in MNCs or similar setups.

S3 — This entrance brings immense prosperity. The occupants of such a house become smarter and their work gets done easily.

S4 — Industries in such plots are highly successful. The family residing in such a space is blessed with more sons.

S5 — People living in such houses are rarely free from debts. They feel incapable of making good use of their intellect.

S6 — A door of abysmal poverty.

S7 — People residing in such houses suffer, as their efforts towards a profession or relationship keep going waste. They remain discontented and unhappy.

S8 — The most ominous entrance, it results in such behaviour and attitude, which gradually disconnects the family from the rest of the world, thereby severely affecting their finances and relationships.

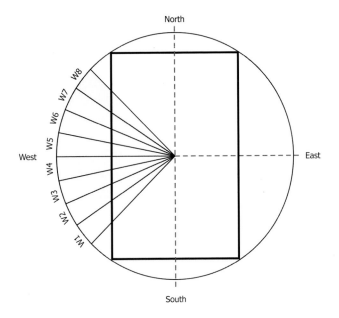

**Possible Entrance Locations in
the Western Segment of a Rectangular Plot**

W1 — This entrance is negative for the residents' financial position and life span.

W2 — This entrance creates instability in career. People residing here lack clarity of thought and vision. They turn insecure, especially of their near and dear ones.

W3 — This entrance brings astounding growth and prosperity.

W4 — It offers no particular benefits or harms. Life in such houses is generally smooth. Overall, it's a good entrance.

W5 — This entrance makes one a perfectionist to the extent of becoming delusional and overambitious. One starts expecting unrealistic gains.

W6 — This entrance makes people prone to mental depression.

W7 — An entrance in this zone causes loss of general happiness in the house. At times, it induces the person to resort to drugs and alcohol.

W8 — This entrance affects the mentality of residents in such a way that they do not mind adopting unfair and unlawful means for their own benefit.

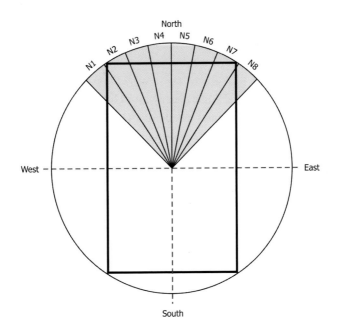

**Possible Entrance Locations in
the Northern Segment of a Rectangular Plot**

N1 — In such a house, the inhabitants become susceptible to harm caused by bad intentions of other people.

N2 — A fear of enemies, that is not entirely unfounded, stalks people living in such houses. Residents feel that others are jealous of them.

N3 — This door brings lots of money and male progeny for those who occupy it.

N4 — This entrance ensures abundance of money, inherited and/or earned.

N5 — This entrance makes people religious, non-aggressive and calm.

N6 — The entrance makes residents behave in a manner that people generally disapprove of. People usually avoid listening to them.

N7 — This entrance instigates rebellious attitude among young girls of the house and makes them go against the family's cultural and social beliefs. In the Indian context, a girl in such a family may resort to an inter caste marriage.

N8 — Such an entrance paves way for a higher bank balance for its occupants.

Once you have determined the location of an entrance through the *MahaVastu*™ method, you will find it easy to match the symptoms occurring in your life with those mentioned in this book. The theories mentioned in *MahaVastu*™ are a refined version of those mentioned in *Vishwakarma Prakash*. Some modifications were made to the original concept, after carefully observing 2,000 practical case studies. Till date, over 10,000 case studies have illustrated the practicality of the *MahaVastu*™ concept, and yet no deviations have been reported.

Once the symptoms are found to be matching hundred per cent with those mentioned in *MahaVastu*™, then by using the 16 techniques of *MahaVastu*™, which basically involve *MahaVastu*™ Theory of Five Elements (normally, in the form of colours, or/and metals), the negative effects of that entrance can be nullified. The effects of the entrance are always very powerful, whether positive or negative. For analysing the effects, you should understand how to identify the entrance location on the plan (made to scale) of a given Space. For this you need to first, note down the directions of the Space and mark them on the map accurately. After that, the symptoms must be matched with those given above. Only then, will you be able to remove the ill-effects of the bad entrance.

The 16 *MahaVastu*™ Zones — The Powers that Govern Your Life

As soon as a piece of land is enclosed within a boundary, it begins to behave like a scaled-down model of the Universe. Various powers come into play from different directions. *MahaVastu*™ classifies these energies and powers into 16 types termed as the 16 *MahaVastu*™ zones. The concept of *MahaVastu*™ zones has been adapted from the *Vedic Vastu Shastra*, repeatedly observed, scientifically applied, experienced and also modified to suit contemporary needs of today's buildings.

(प्राची क्रमेण) ईशान्यां देवतागृहं आग्नेयां पाक मुच्यते ।
नैऋत्यां तु शस्त्रागारं वायव्ये भण्डार संस्थितम् ।।

North-East (NE) is the zone of the Gods (Dev tattva);
South-East (SE) is meant for cooking, namely, kitchen;
South-West (SW) is the zone for keeping tools;
North-West (NW) zone is meant for granary storage;

पूर्वस्यां तु सभागारं दक्षिणे शयनं तथा ।
पश्चिमे भोजनं चैव उत्तरे निधि संस्थितम् ।।

East is the zone of social gathering and meetings;
South zone is for relaxing and sleeping;
West is the zone for dining;
North is the zone of treasure, denoting opportunities and money;

आग्नेय पूर्वयोर्मध्ये दधि मन्थन मन्दिरम् ।
अग्नि प्रेतेश्योर्मध्ये आज्यगेहं प्रशस्यते ।।

East-South-East (ESE) zone is meant for churning (in older times, it
was used for making butter by churning curd);
South-South-East (SSE) is the zone for keeping 'Ghee' (clarified butter)
a source of strength and vigour for the body;

याम्यनैर्ऋत्योर्मध्ये पुरीषत्याग मन्दिरम् ।
नैर्ऋत्याम्बुपयोर्मध्ये विद्याभ्यास मन्दिरम् ।।

South-South-West (SSW) zone is meant for the toilet;
West-South-West (WSW) zone is meant for children's study table;

पश्चिमवायव्योर्मध्ये रोदनार्थं गृहं स्मृतम् ।
पा**प्णो**तरपोर्गेणे गतिगेतं गशास्राते ।।

West–North–West (WNW) is the zone for detoxification;
North–North–West (NNW) is the zone for placing a bedroom to
enjoy sex;

उत्तरेशानयोर्मध्ये औषधार्थं तु कारयेत् ।
नैर्ऋत्यां सूतिका गेहं नृपाणां भूतिमिच्छता ।।
आसन्नप्रसवे मासि कुर्याच्चैव विशेषतः ।
तद्वत् प्रसवकाले स्यादिति शास्त्रेषुनिश्चयः ।।

North–North–East (NNE) zone is meant for medicines;
To ensure easy and safe delivery, the expecting mother should sleep in the
South–West (SW) zone, at least, in the last month of the delivery;
Plan the rest of the things according to the will of the king, namely, the
owner of the building.
- Vishwakarma Prakash (2.93 – 2.99)

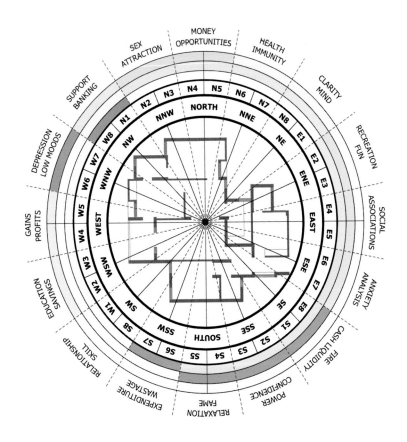

MahaVastu™ Shakti Chakra - **16 Power Zones**

MahaVastu™ divides a building plan into 16 power zones; each covering 22.5° *(refer to the Figure above).*

VASTU ZONE	ATTRIBUTE(S)	ELEMENT	IDEAL ACTIVITY
N	Money and Opportunities	Water	Bedroom
NNE	Health and Immunity	Water	Bedroom
NE	Clarity and Mind	Water	Meditation
ENE	Recreation and Fun	Air	Drawing Room
E	Social Associations	Air	Drawing Room
ESE	Anxiety and Analysis	Air	Toilet
SE	Cash	Fire	Kitchen
SSE	Power and Confidence	Fire	Kitchen
S	Rest, Relaxation and Fame	Fire	Bedroom
SSW	Expenditure and Wastage	Earth	Toilet
SW	Relationship and Skills	Earth	Study
WSW	Education and Savings	Space	Study
W	Gains and Profits	Space	Drawing Room
WNW	Depression	Space	Store
NW	Support and Banking	Earth	Store
NNW	Attraction and Sex	Water	Bedroom

Each of the 16 *MahaVastu*™ zones has its own attributes and effects. Each zone is governed by its specific element, as seen in the table. Balancing of each zone offers an easy path to achieve the desired goals.

The Different Powers of the 16 *MahaVastu*™ Zones

Have you ever noticed that you feel quite relaxed and sleepy in one particular bedroom of your home, but if you sleep in another, you are not able to sleep well? Your children prefer to study at some place other than their study room? Or your expenses shoot up dramatically as soon as you change the placement of your money-safe to a specific area of the house? Family feuds crop up over trifling issues; you put in best efforts, yet the desired results go on eluding you and so on.

The basic reason behind such occurrences lies in the 16 *MahaVastu*™ zones of your home that decide and generate each and every emotion or thought that crops up inside of you. The kind of objects that are placed in a zone and the activities that take place in it, decide the end effect on your corresponding emotions.

If you have a bedroom in the zone of anxiety (ESE), you will never feel relaxed in it. In fact you will notice frequent disagreements cropping up with your spouse. Similarly, your children will get inclined towards studies and will do well academically, if their study table is placed in the zone of education (WSW). Likewise, if there is a toilet in the zone of gains (W), you will never get the expected results. Let us now take a look at these zones and their powers, and their influence on your life.

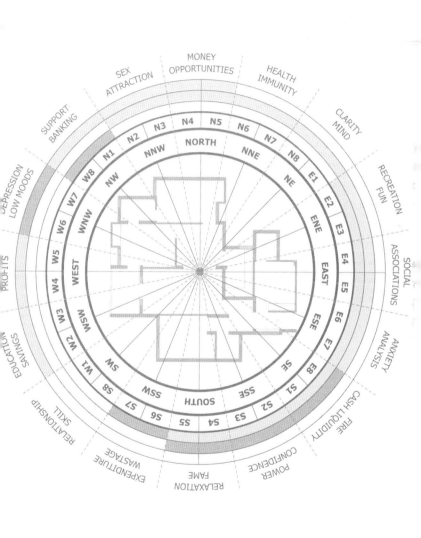

North-East (NE)

Zone of Clarity and Mind

It is the zone of wisdom and meditation. Foresight, intuition, vision, inspiration — all these come from this zone. It is the ideal zone for meditation.

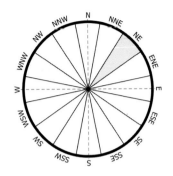

East of North-East (ENE)

Zone of Recreation

Energy from this zone eliminates negativity and infuses positive thoughts and vitality in your mind. It also governs the fun and refreshment in your life. This zone is ideal location for a family lounge.

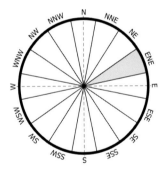

East (E)

Zone of Social Associations

To live your life meaningfully, you need cooperation of your fellow beings, be it at work, at play or at home. The energy generated by the East zone facilitates this social connectivity. It is the ideal zone for the drawing room.

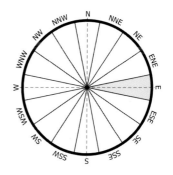

East of South-East (ESE)

Zone of Anxiety

The energy of this zone imparts depth to your thoughts and gives you a deeper understanding of things. If depressed, this zone results in thoughtlessness, and therefore fruitless action. When overactive, this zone lets you have only thoughts but no action. It is the ideal zone for washing laundry.

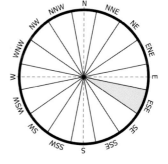

South-East (SE)

Zone of Cash

This zone is also known as the Fire zone. The energy of this zone adds zeal, courage and vigour in your life. The availability of liquid money is the result of the energy of this zone. It is the ideal zone for placing a cash counter.

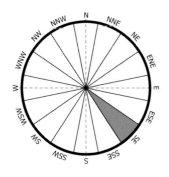

South of South-East (SSE)

Zone of Power and Confidence

If this zone is depressed, its occupants will suffer lack of strength, stamina, vigour and vitality. They will stay bogged down by lethargy, lack of enthusiasm, poor self-confidence and so on. It is the ideal zone for the kitchen.

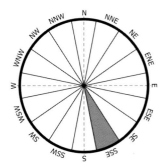

South (S)

Zone of Rest, Relaxation and Fame

This zone helps you re-energise the body and mind after a hard day's work. Most importantly, this is the zone of fame, recognition and social reputation. According to *Mahavastu*™, the master bedroom should be placed in this zone.

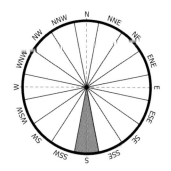

South of South-West (SSW)

Zone of Expenditure and Wastage

The energy of this zone helps you get rid of all waste and useless things in life. Weakness of this zone results in wastage of time, money and efforts on unimportant things, fruitless thoughts, functions and discussions. It is the best zone for the toilet.

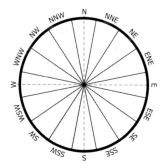

South-West (SW)

Zone of Relationships and Skills

It is the zone of skills, marriage, family harmony, bonding, stability in life and relationships. This zone also awakens your latent and dormant talents. Display all your degrees, certificates and awards in this zone to enhance your skills. It is the ideal zone for placing a work station.

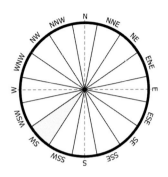

West of South-West (WSW)

Zone of Education and Savings

The West of South-West is the zone of studies, practicing of skills *(vidya abhyaas)*, of knowledge, education, assistance and savings. If this zone is balanced, it ensures greater returns and improved performance with less effort. It is the ideal zone for children's bedroom.

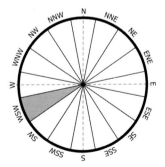

West (W)

Zone of Gains and Profits

The energy of this zone ensures that no action or effort is wasted. It gives you the energy to work tirelessly, and the agility to work with speed. The energy of this zone is like food to the body. It is the ideal zone for a dining hall.

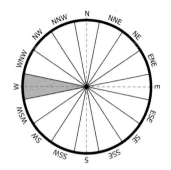

West of North-West (WNW)

Zone of Depression

It is the zone of *rodhan*, that is, stress-release. By merely spending 10 to 15 minutes in this zone, you can free yourself from the negative effects of the past, which otherwise lead to hypertension, stress and depression. It is the ideal zone for keeping a dust bin.

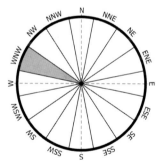

North-West (NW)
Zone of Support and Banking

This is the zone which enables you to garner help or support for future use. In earlier times, the granary used to be in this zone. The North-West zone generates the energy that attracts support and helpful people for any cause you pursue. It is the ideal zone for the storeroom.

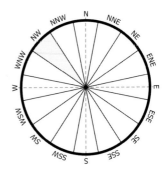

North of North-West (NNW)
Zone of Attraction and Sex

This is the zone of attraction or *rati*, which means sensual enjoyment and a sense of fulfilment. The energy generated by this zone strengthens the bond between a husband and wife. Thus it is the zone of marital bliss, ideal for the bedroom of newly-wed couple.

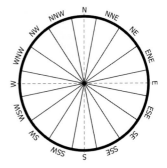

North (N)

Zone of Money and Opportunities

Since the North zone represents money or treasure, its energy helps generate new opportunities to earn money. Placing the bedroom in this zone will be favourable for children's career and opportunities. An imbalance of this zone creates shortage of money and abysmally disproportionate returns for your capabilities and talents.

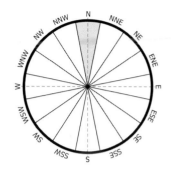

North Of North-East (NNE)

Zone of Health and Immunity

The zone of health ensures balance between physical and mental health. If this zone is disturbed, your body resistance and immune system weakens, making you prone to illnesses. It is the ideal zone for keeping medicines.

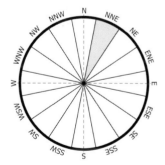

In a particular building, these zonal powers may become overactive or inactive, due to an imbalance of the *Panchtattva*s or the five elements. Such an imbalance adversely affects lives of the people occupying that building.

By using appropriate colours, metals, shapes, symbols and other techniques of *MahaVastu*™, these zones can be balanced in a living space. These zones can in fact be programmed in such a way that they start generating the desired results for you in life.

MahaVastu™ Programming — Symbols and *Panchkosha*s

Manifest Your Dream Life

Symbols are powerful and have their own language and effects. They have been old friends of mankind, guiding and supporting the process of human evolution. Right from ancient times, mans' life has remained strongly connected and related with symbols. Symbols are the formulators *(sutradhar)* of the conscious and the subconscious mind and have been handled with great care. Man possessed the knowledge of symbols from its early ancestors. According to linguists, our fundamental languages were developed from symbols, and they remain an integral part of our life and our mind, even today. The human subconscious mind only understands the language of symbols.

The arena of the subconscious mind is in two domains — one, the subconscious mind of a being, and second, the inner space of a building. The human mind shapes itself according to the space it lives in — the space inside of a building. The philosophy of *MahaVastu*™ believes that *bhawna* (emotion and intention) is the daughter of *bhavana* (building). Emotion and intention are thus the driving forces of your life.

The centre of the entire human existence is the subconscious mind. It is this subconscious which governs and manages the infinite processes of the body — from blood pressure to heartbeat. Even the processes that we remain unaware of throughout our lives are run smoothly and deftly by our subconscious mind.

The analogy of computers serves as the best example, with which we can understand the working process of the conscious and the subconscious minds. Consider this: the conscious mind is the monitor, and the subconscious mind, the Central Processing Unit (CPU).

The CPU works according to the information registered on the monitor — it does not perform any analysis on its own. The language of the CPU is altogether of a different type. Ninety-five per cent of the computer users do not understand the language of the CPU, although it is used to programme the computers. A computer programme is like a set of instructions, written in a particular language which only the CPU can understand. Similarly, the conscious mind gathers information through the five senses (eyes, ears, nose, tongue, skin). It derives information from the pictures it sees through the eyes in the form of paintings and colours, the sounds it hears through the ears, the touch it senses from different textures that come in contact with the skin. All the different objects in the external world create a complex language for the subconscious mind. Information picked unknowingly by the subconscious mind creates the life you actually live. The basis of the *MahaVastu*™ remedies is an understanding of this language and using it to manifest the desired life.

Placed in a building, a symbol has a significant meaning — it says something to our subconscious mind which then begins to act accordingly. The symbols around us stimulate the natural powers of the Earth, to begin the special process of the fulfillment of our desires. Once these powers sense our desires, they begin to programme our subconscious mind accordingly. Thus, the powers lead us to the achievement of our goals. By placing the appropriate symbol in the appropriate *MahaVastu*™ zone (one related to our wish), we can programme our space to fulfill our desires. For example, to achieve a loving relationship with your spouse, you should put the symbol of love birds in the *Vastu* zone of relationships. Your space will get to know what you want and you and your spouse will subconsciously start behaving in a manner which is surprisingly conducive to a cordial and loving relationship. *MahaVastu*™ is unique because it helps us read the symbolic messages of the Universe, and take the desired steps to convey our wishes to the Universe through symbols.

*Panchkosha*s — The Five Layers of Existence

The concept of *Panchkosha* is like a nature-made hardware design of Existence which is spread across five layers in which the entire process of existence takes place. In order to achieve that desirable life, you must understand the 'Alchemy of Space' and the art of working with the symbols. Let us start by understanding the five layers of creation. This knowledge will help us understand the phenomenon of life, and also craft it the way we want it to be.

Most of you experience this in your day-to-day life: You respond to a situation in a particular manner, and later on, wonder where that response actually came from! Your response to a particular situation is rooted in the programming of your mind, which in turn is programmed by the 'five layers of space' you live in.

According to *Vedanta*, the entire creation exists in these five layers which are also called the *Panchkosha* or the five layers of existence namely — *Annamaya Kosha, Pranmaya Kosha, Manomaya Kosha, Vigyanmaya Kosha* and *Anandmaya Kosha*. The outermost layer or *Kosha* is the *Annamaya Kosha* — the gross layer of existence.

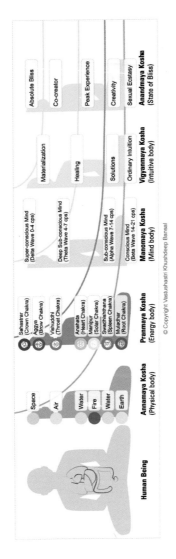

Panchkoshas — The Five Layers of Existence

Human Being

Annamaya Kosha
(Physical body)

Earth
Water
Fire
Water
Air
Space

Pranmaya Kosha
(Energy body)

Muladhar
(Root Chakra)
Swadhishthana
(Spleen Chakra)
Manipur
(Solar Chakra)
Anahata
(Heart Chakra)
Vishuddhi
(Throat Chakra)
Aggya
(Brow Chakra)
Sahastrar
(Crown Chakra)

Manomaya Kosha
(Mind body)

Conscious Mind
(Beta Wave 14-21 cps)
Sub-conscious Mind
(Alpha Wave 7-14 cps)
Deep Sub-conscious Mind
(Theta Wave 4-7 cps)
Super-conscious Mind
(Delta Wave 0-4 cps)

Vigyanmaya Kosha
(Intuitive body)

Ordinary Intuition
Solutions
Healing
Materialization

Anandmaya Kosha
(State of Bliss)

Sexual Ecstasy
Creativity
Peak Experience
Co-creator
Absolute Bliss

© Copyright Vastushastri Khushdeep Bansal

The innermost and the subtlest of all layers is the *Anandmaya Kosha*. The *Annamaya Kosha* is the first layer. Everything that you see in the world is nothing but *Annamaya Kosha*. Thus, every material thing that you see, touch and feel is the *Annamaya Kosha*. Your body, as you see it, is your *Annamaya Kosha*. Interestingly, this concept applies not just to your body, but also to the buildings or the spaces that you see around yourself. Our five senses are also a part of the *Annamaya Kosha,* which is directly connected to the conscious mind. The state of mind in which we experience sense gratification belongs to the *Annamaya Kosha*. According to the Brainwave Theory, this state exhibits the beta brainwave pattern.

Do you wonder what drives the inert *Annamaya Kosha* or the material form of the world that you see? What is the source of energy of the *Annamaya Kosha?* The powerhouse of the *Sthoola Jagat* is an energy body called *Pranmaya Kosha*.

Roughly translated, *prana* means energy. *Pranmaya Kosha* is so important for the *Annamaya Kosha* that the *Taittiriya-Upanishad* describes it as the *atma* of the *Annamaya Kosha*. This is the reason why an individual is commonly called as *Prani* in both the Sanskrit and Hindi languages. When *Prana* has been tamed through *Pranayam,* our mind is quietened. In this state, it becomes most energetic and capable of doing almost unimaginable things. A state of mind which goes beyond the gratification of the five senses controls the energy body, namely the *Pranmaya Kosha*. This lies in between the beta and the alpha brainwave patterns.

In *Yoga* and *Tantra, Pranmaya Kosha* is depicted through *Kundalini, Ida–Pingala (nadi)* and the seven *Chakras*. Traditionally, these *Chakras* are believed to be associated with the human body only; however, the truth is that they also exist in the building structures that we occupy. Nestled inside the *Pranmaya Kosha* is *Manomaya Kosha,* which is subtler than the previous two *Koshas*. It is the soul, the *atma,* of the *Pranmaya Kosha.* The *Prana* which is the vital energy-backup for all your activities (physical, physiological or mental) remains under the control of the *Manomaya Kosha.* This layer is known as the mind-body, or the 'thought' layer of your personality.

There are numerous thoughts that course through your mind every day. These thoughts are triggered by the conditioning of your mind, its likes and dislikes, memories, emotions or even wisdom. One half of the *Manomaya Kosha* is the subconscious mind. Likewise, the rest of the mind connects with the next *Kosha,* the *Vigyanmaya Kosha* — this lies in between the alpha and theta brainwave patterns. All the thoughts born in your mind, meaningful or bizarre, are shaped to a great extent by your space, namely, the buildings where you live or work.

So what is the self of the *Manomaya Kosha?* It is the *Vigyanmaya Kosha.* As the name itself suggests, it is the seat of *Vigyan* or knowledge. What you call intuition or *poorva abhas* comes from this *Vigyanmaya Kosha.* Premonition of things to come, forewarning of some impending trouble or an intuitive feeling that something really good is about to happen — all this originates in *Vigyanmaya Kosha.* It is a deeper layer of human mind which is connected with the super-conscious part of brain — scientifically known as the theta brainwave pattern.

While moving from one *Kosha* to another, you are progressing from the gross to the subtle layers; from the coarse state to the state of perfect bliss. However, nature follows the opposite course — the entire creation originates in that perfect state of bliss. It is from the *Anandmaya Kosha* that all things have emerged.

The root cause of *dukh* or grief is ignorance. Once you are free from the bondage of ignorance, you attain the perfect state of bliss, namely, *Anand*. Therefore, the final and original layer of existence — the layer from which everybody has evolved is the *Anandmaya Kosha*. This is the delta brainwave pattern, where one can consciously experience the super-consciousness and absolute joy or the *Anand*.

Everyone has a desire for *Anand*. Nature achieves its task of creation through this desire. In your quest for *Anand* you, in a certain state of mind, transform your energy into *Annamaya Kosha,* namely, another human body. You are always in search of *Anand* or joy because it is this very state which led to your own creation. That is why you create the *Sthoola Jagat* or the material world to enjoy blissfully every moment in life. It is your basic nature to have such a desire. The order of transition from *Anandmaya Kosha* to *Annamaya Kosha* is reversed when you build a home or any other building. Now, it is through *Sthoola* or the 'material' that you want to achieve subtle bliss.

The ultimate purpose of a building is to achieve *Anand,* whether it is through amassing wealth or through fame. There may be several routes but the sole aim of all your activity is *Anand*. How you actually get that feeling of *Anand* is conditioned by the space you inhabit.

Your space is alive and whatever desires you convey to it, knowingly or unknowingly, start working to manifest them.

This forms the basic *Mantra* of life programming. After recognising your desires clearly, you can programme your energy-body and mind-body layers through *Vastu* to get connected to the *Vigyanmaya* and *Anandmaya Koshas,* to ultimately achieve the life of your dreams. It is only through a healthy balance between the Existence and ourselves that we can ensure good health, abundant wealth and lasting prosperity. An imbalance between the Existence and us is the root cause of all the problems that we face in our day-to-day life.

Understanding the Balance of Nature and the *MahaVastu*™ Programming

MahaVastu™ is dedicated to developing an understanding of — the naturally occurring energies and, the art of balancing energies in our built-up environments. *MahaVastu*™ programming can help you even-out an imbalanced situation, to make it harmonious and balanced. While using *MahaVastu*™ programming, you should be very cautious about the use of symbols. There is a four-step process which is carried out to programme a building's environment in such a way that you achieve the desired results. Placing symbols forms the fourth and the final step, which is followed as a finishing touch to a building. But before we apply the *MahaVastu*™ remedies, the first three steps must be completed.

The first step is to analyse the cycle of creation and the cycle of destruction in order to attain a balance of the five elements.

Second step is to analyse the location of the entrance of a building and correct it if required, through *MahaVastu*™ techniques. Only a correctly placed entrance connects the inner space of a building with the universal space. This process is exactly like connecting a computer to the power supply.

The third step is to evaluate the strengths and the weaknesses of the *Vastu* zones in your built-up space or building. Remember: the power generated by these zones is instrumental in shaping your life situations. Unless you have completed these three steps, the fourth step alone (of using symbols) will not work properly.

To use and apply *MahaVastu*™ programming, one must analyse the root *Kosha* with which the problems are connected (the concept of *Panchkosha*s has been explained earlier in the book). To solve the problems related with the *Annamaya Kosha;* restoring the elemental balance and correcting the entrance effects is sufficient. For problems pertaining to the *Pranmaya Kosha* and *Manomaya Kosha,* the application of '*MahaVastu*™ *Shakti Chakra*' will get the desired solutions. The issues related with the higher levels — the *Manomaya Kosha* and *Vigyanmaya Kosha* — can be addressed by using *MahaVastu*™ programming in combination with the three steps mentioned above.

The *MahaVastu*™ learning ensures that a learner becomes well versed with the identification of the disturbed *kosha*s, which are the root cause of all problems. Once the disturbed *kosha*s are identified by analysing and evaluating an existing building, the remedial measures can be carried out using the 16 *MahaVastu*™ techniques. You must thoroughly understand the above-mentioned concepts and their practical observations before you decide a course of action aimed at achieving the desired results.

Do not be hasty, remember — nature takes her own course and works at her own pace, but she is far more effective than we can imagine. Moreover, if you need to address more than one problem in a given time, it is advisable to deal with them one by one. The same holds true for wishes and desires you may want to fulfill.

Never try to set everything right at the same time. Prioritise your wants, and work accordingly. You will notice that very often, a single problem has many manifestations. In such a case, treating one of these manifestations usually eliminates the problem and all its various forms. Applying too many remedies in one go may also cause imbalance. So, deal with only one problem at a time. If you feel that the situation is too complicated, then consult an experienced *MahaVastu*™ expert before you proceed.

The following are some of the symbols which, when used judiciously, can completely transform your life.

Increase Money Flow with Kuber

Yaksharaj Kuber is the Lord of Wealth and the guardian of all the treasures in the Universe. He is responsible for all the money transactions involving your efforts and work. He also presents to you new opportunities, in case you are not satisfied with your current income. To ensure the right money-

flow in your home or to avail new opportunities in your career, place a statue of Kuber on a table or on a shelf in a wall in the North (N) *MahaVastu*™ zone of the building. Do not worship Kuber*ji* with incense sticks or Deepak as a Yaksha is not worshipped.

Enhance Self-confidence and Power with the Lion

To enhance your confidence-level in situations where you lack it, and to develop a powerful self-presence, place a brass lion on the floor in the North-North-East (NNE) *MahaVastu*™ zone of your home. Make sure that the lion faces the Centre of the building.

Your dear ones will notice an immediate change in you You will be stronger, more gracious and possessing a more powerful personality.

Get Support from Government Departments with the Ashoka Pillar

When placed in the North-West (NW) *MahaVastu*™ zone, the Ashoka Pillar guarantees government support and yields exceptional results in areas pertaining to government favours, promotion and recognition. Do not place the Ashoka Pillar anywhere between the South-East (SE) and South (S) areas of your house — since this will invite harassment by a government department or official, allegations and prosecutions.

Command the Power of the Sun

As per *MahaVastu*™, the Sun represents the governing or the ruling power. It also helps you get the wisdom and skills to build fruitful associations that spread your glory, name and reputation all around. To create a powerful effect, the Sun should be placed in a hanging position in the East (E) *MahaVastu*™ zone of your home — at a height of seven feet from the floor. Do not put a Sun face which is showing an expression of pain, stress or anger. Pick the one looking solemn, earnest, gentle, benevolent and smiling graciously.

Victory With Sword

The Sword was widely used as a *Vastu* remedy in ancient India. Even today, you will find swords placed graciously on the walls of Indian palaces and homes belonging to people in power. Its main use was and still is ensuring victory. This victory may be in the form of increased profits, winning court cases,

political battles or even in getting coveted contracts. To win a court case, display a Sword on the wall that lies in the East-North-East (ENE) *MahaVastu*™ zone of the building.

Fulfil Wishes with the Kamdhenu Cow

As per the *Puranic* tales, the Kamdhenu Cow was one of the 14 gems that came out when the gods and the demons churned the oceans. When placed on the floor, in the East-South-East (ESE) *MahaVastu*™ zone, the Kamdhenu Cow converts the energy responsible for contemplation, worry and inner conflicts into productive and fruitful action, thereby assisting you in fulfillment of your wishes.

Accelerate flow of work with a pair of Red Horses

When placed in the South (S) *MahaVastu*™ zone, a pair of galloping Red Horses sparks off steady flow of work. This kind of work always brings in more fund flow, fame and repeated business orders. However, make sure that you use this *MahaVastu*™ remedy after clearing the North (N) and South-  East (SE) zones of useless articles. The statue may be placed either on the floor or in an almirah in the South (S) zone. Its face should always be towards North.

Reap more Benefits from Business Relationships with Rabbits

Rabbits make secret underground tunnels and run very fast. Do you desire progress in ventures and truly believe that good relationships are the secret of growth, but are not able to receive benefits at the right time? By placing a pair of black and white brass Rabbits, you can reap higher profits in business relationships at the right time. The Rabbits should be placed on the floor in the East-South-East (ESE) *MahaVastu*™ zone of your home.

Sharpen your Skills with Garuda

Lord Vishnu governs the whole Universe. Garuda is Lord Vishnu's trusted mount and attendant. Garuda functions as God's tool to maintain the Universe. Garuda looks like an eagle with a human head and hands. So, Garuda represents a combination of sharp foresight and action with human intelligence and consciousness. To sharpen your skills and to control your inner and outer systems in a better way, place Garuda in the South-West (SW) *MahaVastu*™ zone.

Stop Wastages with a Yellow Vase

A yellow earthen vase placed on the floor or on a table, in the South-South-West (SSW) *MahaVastu*™ zone of your building gives way to stability. This object brings down unnecessary expenditure and encourages saving, thus, increasing the profits. The yellow vase also puts an end to the dissipation and 'wearing-away' of vitality, health and relationships by providing you strength and power.

Strengthen the Bond of Love with Love Birds

This symbolic object curbs out misunderstandings, discontentment and tensions that arise from petty issues and is very effective in developing a loving relationship between married couples. Love birds are also helpful if you are looking for a soul mate or life-partner. In case your child is of marriageable  age, place the love birds in the South-West (SW) zone of his or her bedroom. This will ensure that your child finds an ideal life partner.

Improve Education and Grades with the Swastika Symbol

Every ancient civilisation in India carried the Swastika symbol in one form or the other. By merely drawing a Swastika symbol in a space, you can synchronise it with the Universal mind. Drawing the Swastika symbol in a zone harmonises it with the universal  consciousness. The Swastika will connect your children's consciousness with knowledge and education. Drawing the symbol of a Swastika in the West-South-West (WSW) *MahaVastu*™ zone helps children perform better in their studies.

Become a Smarter Player in your Business with the Chessboard

If you are unable to achieve the right targets, even though you have utilised all your resources, skill-sets, knowledge and opportunities, then try placing a chessboard in the West (W) *MahaVastu*™ zone as it will awaken your latent talents. The chessboard enables you to perform excellently at the right time and the right place.

Become More Active and Alert with the Deer

Place a Deer statue on the floor or table in the West-North-West (WNW) *MahaVastu*™ zone of your home. It infuses vitality and speed into sluggish system and has the ability to smoothen out seriously tangled situations. The Deer not only lends greater speed to a system, but also ensures that the entailed work is skillfully done. It also increases coordination among those involved in a company/venture.

Get Financial Support with White Horses

To acquire the most fruitful support from your bank in terms of financial matters, loans and overdrafts, place a pair of White Horses statues in the North-West (NW) *MahaVastu*™ zone, on the floor or in an almirah. Horse symbolises speed and the white colour, excellent quality. White Horses in the

zone of support improve access to banks and financial institutions, ensuring that your support systems reposes complete faith in you and your company. Make sure the White Horses' head faces the South-East (SE) direction.

Amplify Positivity with a Pyramid

Pyramids are very powerful and therefore, must be used with great care. They amplify a zone's energy by approximately 108 times. When placed in the North (N), the Pyramid enhances the energy responsible for bringing in money. In the North-North-East (NNE) *MahaVastu*™ zone, it promotes

health and in the North-East (NE) zone, it awakens wisdom and awareness. Always place the Pyramid on the floor and align it along the North-South axis. It must never be stuck on a wall, door or ceiling as this can have dangerous effects.

3. *Vastu* Myths Busted

All knowledge has only one purpose — to provide you with the betterment of life and the ability to live in complete joy. The knowledge which cannot be applied, or which does not take you towards the light of wisdom and insights, will only lead to darkness and ignorance. It is ignorance which becomes a hindrance in achieving whatever you want in your life. It acts as a hurdle in the way of good life, achievement of desires and dreams.

Through practical observations and scientific usage of *MahaVastu*™ procedures, we realised that there are several myths about *Vastu* which exist and create problems for those unaware of the truth. These myths create confusions, making it impossible to apply the real knowledge of *Vastu*. The knowledge of *Vastu* is not new, since it has been with us for the past 12,000 years.

You can verify the application of this knowledge in monuments and excavations by the archaeological departments, not only in India, but throughout the world. The documentation of this knowledge that we have with us today dates back to BC 500 - 1200 AD.

Ever since man became conscious of his environment and its effects on his being (effects that control his emotions, intentions, consciousness, and in physical form — his health) he also began to explore the effects of Earth's energies on him and the space configurations around him. From the time when humans lived in caves, till today, human consciousness has gone through a complex phenomenon. It evolved at a very slow pace from BC 500 - 1200 AD. During 1200 AD - 1800 AD, there was a different kind of evolution in human consciousness.

In this era, different systems/models of thought developed in the form of new sects and cults. The traditional and newly-developed thought models concerning codes of living, which we call 'religion', created different kind of lifestyles and philosophies for the conduct of life. Apart from this, the climatic factors too molded people's view of nature and fashioned their lifestyles. As a combined result of all these effects, the living environments changed. However, the core philosophies continued to reflect the same knowledge that human consciousness had ingrained from environment ages ago. In the last 200 years, it is not only the human mind and consciousness that has evolved to a different scale, but also the complex lifestyles of present times. Over the past 20 years only, mankind has witnessed phenomenal change across each and every aspect of life. And all this happened is just 20 years! Taking all these facts into consideration, we need to re-evaluate our models of thought and perception. We must do away with the myths that have no scientific or rational basis/understanding. The word 'scientific' used here refers to any phenomenon and/or practical knowledge that can unerringly and repeatedly yield the same results, using the same formulae or established set of observations. We might not be able to explain the laws working behind a concept but we can certainly verify the truth, after we have continuous observations and desired results attained through its application.

MahaVastu™ experts are open to every kind of knowledge that can be observed, verified and finally used to create a better life for everyone on the planet. With this understanding, we are going to openly de mystify some of the most common myths from one of the most scientifically tested and useful knowledge bases of life — *MahaVastu*™. These myths caused lots of confusions and created hindrances in achieving the benefits of *Vastu.*

- Believe it or Not
  - Lord Ganesha at the Entrance

Importance of
Accuracy of Directions
- *Puja* in the North-East

Study Facing East
- Adjoining Kitchen and Toilet
  - Three Doors in a Straight Line

Anti-Clockwise Stairs
- Entrance in the West or South Directions
- Toilet in the North Direction

- Marriageable girls should not sleep in the North-West direction
  - Auspicious Basements
Dressing Table Reflecting the Bed
- Square Plots

Believe it or Not

The most widely held misconception about *Vastu* is that you must have complete faith in it to reap its amazing benefits. The fact, however, is that *Vastu* is a completely scientific discipline. Like other sciences, the outcomes of *Vastu* techniques are not affected by your lack or absence of faith in them.

Since time immemorial, man has been conscious of the tremendous influence that nature and earth exert in shaping his life. That is why all human civilisations have referred to them as 'mother'. Since man has an inquisitive and scientific temperament, he developed through meditation, intuition and systematic observations, an understanding of the energies associated with the Earth. The directions of their flow and how these Earth energies influence him have been codified into knowledge bases. On the basis of this knowledge, man developed the science of *Vastu* — the science of planning building structures of all kinds. The sole aim of *Vastu* is to help a building materially achieve the purpose for which it has been built. Clearly, *Vastu* is concerned with the flow of Earth energies, which is an independent phenomenon having nothing to do with anybody's faith. It works with the right placements of the appropriate objects in the appropriate locations.

Lord Ganesha at the Entrance

Placing a figurine of Lord Ganesha at the entrance of homes, offices, shops and other buildings has been in vogue since a long time. Most people believe that it is inauspicious to place a Lord Ganesha image or a statue which has its back towards their home. So, they place another image on the inside of the entrance. In this way, the position of *Sarvapratham Pujaniya* Lord Ganesha is reduced to that of a mere *dwarpal* or gatekeeper. Moreover, by placing Ganesha image both inside and outside of the wall, they unknowingly face his back whenever they enter or leave the building. This practice must be avoided at any cost since it brings abject poverty *(daaridrya)* to the occupants of such a building.

Interestingly, this tradition had started in Rajasthan about 250 years ago. This region, which used to be in ancient times one of the most prosperous regions in the country, today has been branded a *bimar rajya* or a sick state, officially by the government.

There is another reason behind not displaying Lord Ganesha's image at the entrance. According to a tale mentioned in the Hindu scriptures, Goddess Parvati had asked Lord Ganesha to guard the entrance while she was busy inside. Following her instructions, Lord Ganesha did not allow anybody in, even stopping her husband Lord Shiva at the door. This enraged Lord Shiva and a severe clash happened between the two. Since then, the belief has prevailed that Lord Ganesha should not be placed at the entrance.

Importance of Accuracy of Directions

The basic foundation of *Vastu* rests on the flow of energies in various directions, yet, surprisingly enough — the directions remain the most neglected aspect of *Vastu* today. Even in the rare cases where directions are taken into account, the analysis is done wrongly — without sparing any thought to actual geographical directions. As a result, people misinterpret and wrongly use *Vastu Yantra*s, subjecting buildings to major and costly changes which yield no benefit to its occupants at all. These misinterpreted ventures lead into people dismissing *Vastu* as mere mumbo jumbo.

MahaVastu™ clearly specifies the importance of direction through what are called the *Vastu* zones. While a line represents a direction, a *Vastu* zone denotes the expansion-limits of a direction — 11.25° on either side of the line drawn from the centre of the space. If we divide the total built-up space (360° around the centre) into 16 equal parts of 22.5° each *(refer to Figure on page 34)*, then each part can be called a *MahaVastu*™ zone. These zones govern specific aspects of your life.

It is the practicality and the compatibility of *MahaVastu*™ with all kinds of dimensions and spaces, that it is considered the most scientific, rational and accurate method of *Vastu* analysis.

Puja in the North-East

A widely followed myth is that the act of worshipping or *puja* should be performed in the *Ishaan* or the North-East (NE) direction only. However, if you observe old palaces or old homes made exactly as per the *Vastu Shastra, puja* altars remain situated in the West zone of the building. Moreover, in all the temples, deities are placed in the West, with their face towards the East direction. To understand this concept better, let us review what is written in the *Vastu Shastra (refer to page 34).* The scriptures say *"Ishaanyam Devtagriham"* meaning *Devta*s or deities reside in the North-East *Vastu* zone. However, the scriptures do not say that one must worship or do *puja* in this particular zone. Had the writer of *Vishwakarma Prakash* meant otherwise, while mentioning the ideal activities of different *Vastu* zones in the same series of shlokas, he would have written — *Pujagraham* instead of *Devtagriham.* The word *Dev* means a deity or a soul guide with whom you communicate in a meditative state. This North-East zone governs clarity of thoughts and intuitive foresights, helping you gain benefits in life. Therefore, *Devta*s or deities' idols or paintings may be placed here. However, the rituals or the worshipping should not be performed in this zone. To perform rituals, one can choose any of the adjoining *Vastu* Zones — NNE and ENE, since both these zones support the processes of cleansing and strengthening of the *Manomaya* and *Vigyanmaya Kosha*s. As per *MahaVastu*™, different deities reside in different directions and govern varied aspects of our lives. To get the blessings of a deity, one must worship or offer *puja* in the particular direction which is governed by that deity. For example, *puja* of Lord Hanuman and Goddess Mother Durga should be performed in South (S) zone only. Similarly, one should place the *puja* altars of different *Devta*s in the 16 *Vastu* zones as per the respective zones governed by them.

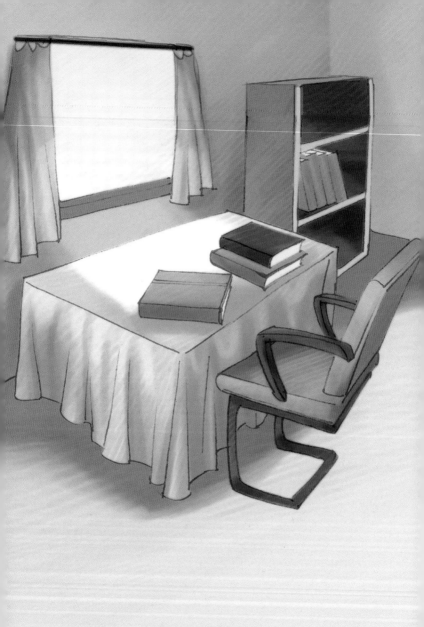

Study Facing East

Growing up as school kids in India, almost all of us have some memories about our parents, friends and other well-wishers telling us to study facing the East. The fact, however, is that there is no one direction that is suitable for all fields of study. The 'most suitable direction' actually depends on the subject that is being studied. For example, to achieve proficiency in Mathematics and Science, students should study facing the West. If one studies facing the South, he develops good debating skills, logical ability and sharp business acumen. When studying creative or religious works, one should study facing the East. These days, the most common issue that the parents face regarding children is that they do not pay much attention to studies. For such children, the study table should be set up in the middle of the South-West and West. If this arrangement is not possible, then try the following alternative zones for setting up the study — North-East (NE); South-East (SE) and South (S). If children do not concentrate on their books and are frequently distracted, they should study facing the West.

Adjoining Kitchen and Toilet

It is a common misconception that a kitchen and a toilet should not be adjoining each other in a building. Surprisingly, the ideal location for toilet and kitchen is the one adjacent to each other, says the *MahaVastu*™ theory of five elements and the *MahaVastu*™ *Shakti Chakra*. As per our own experience and observation of 18 years — none of the adjoining-kitchen-toilet designs followed in thousands of buildings, create any negative effect on anybody.

In fact, the kitchen and the toilet should be built after considering the elements associated with the 16 *MahaVastu* zones. According to *MahaVastu*™, the best Zone for the kitchen is South-East (SE), with other permissible *Vastu* zones being North-West (NW), West (W), South (S) and South-South-East (SSE). On the other hand, *Vastu* zones prescribed for locating the toilet are South-South-West (SSW), West-North-West (WNW), and East-South-East (ESE). Clearly, the ideal location of a kitchen lies adjacent to the ideal locations of a toilet. It should also be remembered that the kitchen is represented by the Fire element and the toilet by Earth. Since the Fire element complements the Earth, there is no mistake or *Vastu dosh* in keeping the kitchen and the toilet adjacent to each other.

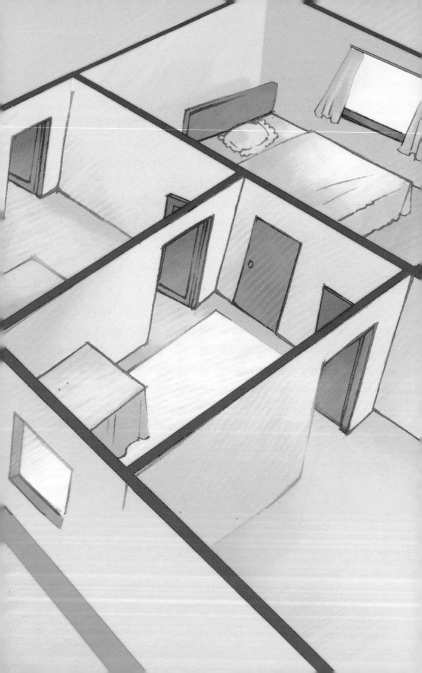

Three Doors in a Straight Line

A common misconception is that *Vastu* does not permit aligning two or more doors facing each other or in a straight line. Also, another commonly-held myth is that the doors should always be staggered. The reality, however, is that all the ancient *Vastu* scriptures are silent about the alignment of doors. The plans of old buildings, including ancient temples, do not support any of these myths. In fact, the four main doors in ancient temples — the main entrance, door to the *prasaad*, the *mandap* door and the door to the *garbha griha* — are always aligned in a straight line.

The straight-line-pattern of doors can also be seen in several houses of Old Delhi. Those houses are beautiful case studies exemplifying the *MahaVastu*™ four-step method. The streets in which these houses are located were in ancient times, the central attraction of the city. Even today, the Old Delhi streets hold a key position, housing one of largest and most flourishing wholesale markets in Asia. If aligning three doors in a single row was so grievously wrong, then this city would not have prospered over the centuries. Thus, it is better to design the doors as per the practical requirements of architecture, keeping them in compliance with the second pillar of *MahaVastu*™, namely, the effects of the 32 entrances.

Anti-Clockwise Stairs

Many people consider anti-clockwise stairs having extremely negative effects. *Vastushastri* Khushdeep Bansal collected a lot of data to clarify whether the stairs should be in clockwise or anti-clockwise direction. Interestingly, in the original texts of *Vastu Shastra* there are no guidelines on staircases. From his own observations, *Vastushastri* Khushdeep Bansal derived a formula which measures the effects of clockwise and anti-clockwise staircases.

As per his observations, a clockwise staircase creates a downward vortex of energy in a *Vastu* zone, while an anti-clockwise staircase creates an upward energy vortex. These downward and upward energy vortices change the natural effect of a *Vastu* zone. The analogy of his concept is this: as you tighten a screw, you rotate the screw driver clockwise and the screw goes downwards. Vice versa, if you rotate the screwdriver in the anti-clockwise direction, it rises up. Therefore, a clockwise staircase in the NE zone will suppress new ideas, creativity and intuitions. On the other hand, an anti-clockwise staircase in the same zone (NE) will create new ideas and creative intuitions. Clockwise staircases in positive zones will suppress their natural positive energy; anti-clockwise ones will amplify the positive energy. So, remember: a staircase can be clockwise as well as anti-clockwise depending upon the *Vastu* zone it falls into.

If the stairs are in a zone whose attributes we wish to enhance (for example, the zone of money) they should be anti-clockwise, and if they are in a zone whose effects we need to moderate, (like the zone of disposal or aggression), they must be clockwise. Generally speaking, a staircase should descend from West to East and from South to North.

Entrance in the West or South Directions

Many people give up the West and the South-facing plots because they are mostly considered inauspicious. The surprising fact is that 80 per cent of the most successful businessmen and political leaders occupy West or South-facing properties. This disproves the fact that the main entrances in the West or South zones are inauspicious.

MahaVastu™ relies on practical observations and case studies whose results are distilled to get a crystal-clear understanding. It was established by over 2,000 documented case studies that the direction towards which a building is facing, has no impact. What's important is the exact location of the entrance of a building, which should be planned after adhering to the directives of the 'Second Pillar of *MahaVastu*™'.

Today, we live in a modern and materialistic world where knowledge, skills, expertise, fame and brand-value are responsible for attracting money.

Attributes like knowledge, skill and expertise are the attributes of the West direction. Fame, recognition and power are attributes of the South direction. So the activities related with these areas of life must be conducted in West and South-facing buildings only.

If you observe famous restaurants and food shops, you will notice that almost all of them must be facing the West. Most of the technological companies and skill-imparting institutions are West-facing. One must know his domain in which he desires to grow and excel. Then, he should check the appropriate zone (out of the 16 zones) which is most conducive to his area of work. Accordingly, for his activities, he must decide the direction that will suit him the best.

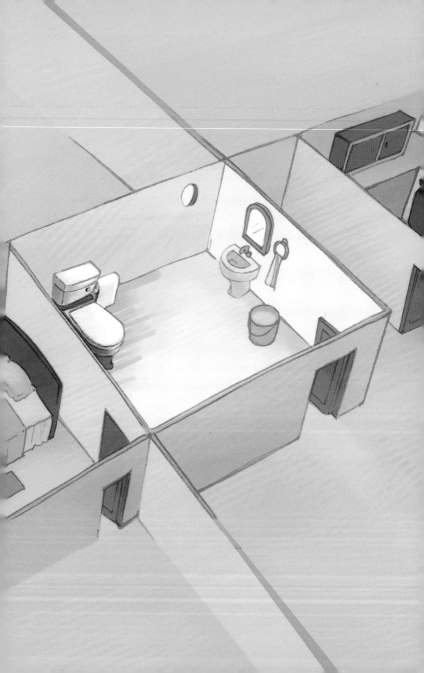

Toilet in the North Direction

Without having proper knowledge of *Vastu*, one cannot decide the correct direction for his various activities in a particular space. Many *Vastu* consultants who do not understand *Vastu* correctly argue that the toilet represents Water element and hence should be placed in the North direction. Even worse, many of the so-called *Vastu* advisors tell people that *Vastu Purusha* is a demon who has his head in the North-East (NE), direction, so the toilet should be placed in the North-East. *MahaVastu*™ experts have visited and corrected this fault in hundreds of such places where a toilet in the North (N) direction was blocking receipt of payments and opportunities. A toilet placed in the North-East (NE) in fact causes neurological problems and even cancer. Doing so hinders the evolution of mind and gives way to chronic diseases and acute depression. In totality, placing a toilet in the NE hampers growth and vision.

The fact is that a toilet represents the act of disposal. Therefore, the ideal place for it is the zone of disposal. If placed in the zone of money and opportunities (North), it will flush out these aspects from your life. It can also be placed in the West-North-West (WNW), which is the zone of depression and low moods. Here, these negative aspects get flushed out from life.

Marriageable girls should not sleep in the North-West direction

The North-West zone is the zone of support and banking. However, it is foolish to think that placing goods here will bring faster commercial movement, or a young unmarried girl sleeping in this zone will get marriage proposals instantly.

MahaVastu™ experts visited the homes of people who claimed that the NW Zone proved lucky for them. What they observed was that the girls sleeping in the NW zone hoping to find suitable match were actually sleeping in the zone of sex and attraction, that is, the North-North-West (NNW). Due to the effects of this zone, the girls though did materialise their dreams of marriage, but soon after, started facing problems in marital life. They faced lack of understanding and indifference from their spouses.

As per *MahaVastu*™, a girl ready for marriage should sleep in the South (S), South-South-East (SSE), South-West (SW) or in the West-South-West (WSW) Zone. Sleeping in the South (S) direction will keep her cool, calm and relaxed. Sleeping in the South-South-East (SSE) will make her more self-confident and healthy. A girl's bedroom in the South-West (SW) zone will make her better skilled in her work and capable of managing good relationship with her spouse. Sleeping in the West-South-West (WSW) direction will give her knowledge and the ability to excel in education. The qualities of these zones will help her find a suitable match, be healthy and skilled, enjoy marital bliss and live a blissful married life. After marriage, the newly married couples can choose the North-North-West (NNW) zone to sleep. However, girls of marriageable age should avoid sleeping in North-West (NW) Zone, since the energy of this zone can harm their reproductive capacity.

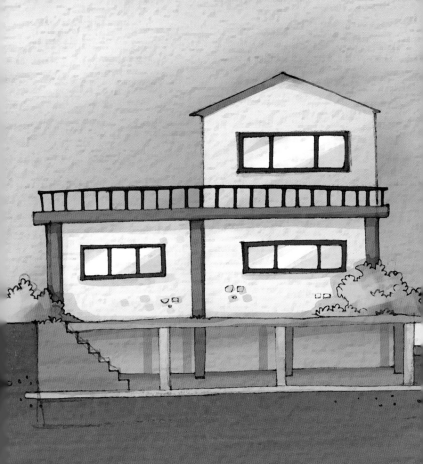

Auspicious Basements

Many a times, people constructing the basement of their house get confused about its *Vastu* needs. Often, people with incomplete knowledge of *Vastu* say that basements are always inauspicious in a home, which, in fact, is not true.

To answer whether or not should you have a basement in your house, *Vastushastri* Khushdeep Bansal analysed hundreds of case studies of the Victorian houses in London which had massive basements. He observed that most of these Victorian homes were actually the most expensive properties of England. This made him wonder, whether there was any truth in basements being inauspicious at all! If they were inauspicious, these properties would not be so expensive or exclusive.

He collected the data from these properties and studied the effects on the inhabitants of such houses. What he found was quite interesting. People who lived in those Victorian houses were the ones responsible for making the British rulers of the world! This made it clear to Khushdeep, that basements do not create negative effects. He also collected data on successful offices and homes that were located in basements. His study inferred what is mentioned in the *MahaVastu*™ *Sutra*, that "if basements were made in the South-facing and West-facing plots, they always created highly positive effects for the occupants".

Basements shall be made in the North and East zones of North and East-facing plots, respectively. Furthermore, a basements being auspicious or inauspicious depends on the location of the entrance and the staircase leading to it.

Dressing Table Reflecting the Bed

Many people consult *MahaVastu*™ experts and tell them that they are confused about the right placement of their dressing table. They fear that having the reflection of their bed in the mirror may bring sleep disorders and misery in relationships.

The truth is: reflection of the bed in the dressing-table-mirror does not create any negative effects by itself. It is the location of the mirror in an incompatible zone that causes the problem. The mirror, as an object, represents Water element. It serves as a medium of extension of space.

Placing a mirror in the South-East direction is like mixing water with fire, South-East being the zone of fire. Since water destroys fire, placing a mirror in the South-East zone will cause negative effects. It could cause accidents and injuries to the inhabitants.

A dressing table in the South-South-West (SSW) zone gives an extension to the zone of disposal. So, it increases wastages and leads to loss of fertility for the people sleeping in those bedrooms.

The zone responsible for causing problems in relationships is the South-West (SW) zone of the home. If a mirror is placed in the South-West zone, then due to its extension effects, problems arise. The couple expect too much from each other. So, one must be careful about placing a mirror in a particular zone.

Square Plots

A square plot being ideal for making a home is a widespread myth. Many people delay making their own home because they are in search of a square plot. In practice, we have found that square plots are found only in villages, where there is plenty of land available. In well-developed and organised urban infrastructure, most plots are rectangular in shape.

A commonly-held belief, that square plots are ideal is actually a myth. People living in perfect-square plots have never been found doing too well in life. *MahaVastu*™ experts tried finding the impact of square plots on its inhabitants with the help of a detailed study — effect of spaces on human consciousness. The *MahaVastu*™ team found that: 'Any perfect space symbolises death, while imperfection makes the world exist.'

As per Hindu mythology, the Earth rests on the hood of the *Shesh-Naag*. This symbolic representation depicts the survival and evolution of life. '*Shesh*' in Sanskrit means residue and '*Naag*' means serpent, making *Shesh-Naag* a depiction of 'serpent energy'. If we decode the symbolism, the serpent energy is found residing inside the human body in the form of *Kundalini*. This pushes the residue (the seed and ovum) to create life on the planet.

Life is created out of the desire to achieve the *Anandmaya Kosha*. Those individuals, who took their consciousness to a different state/ stage of completion, lost interest in creating a new life. So, as per *Vastu Shastra,* perfect square-shaped buildings are recommended only for meditation centres and religious practices, not homes and business places. Therefore, it is always better to have rectangular plots for homes.

4. Working with *MahaVastu*™

Practical case studies

The four steps of *MahaVastu*™ offer the most comprehensive, logical, scientific and practical approach to have solutions for everyday problems. This makes *MahaVastu*™ the world's best *Vastu* method. It provides solutions and gives greater flexibility to architectural designs of apartments, bungalows and every other type of building.

In the *MahaVastu*™ training programme, the first phase or the first two days are devoted to teaching every participant the practical applications with in-depth understanding of the core principles and fundamentals of *Vastu*. From the following case studies, it will be clear how the Four Step *MahaVastu*™ brings results and helps you to live the life your desire.

Receiving the Best Opportunities in Career

Aarti was a very good teacher. Every student who took tuitions from her was very happy with her teaching. Each class that Aarti conducted had such clarity that students barely needed any repetitions of the same lesson ever again. However, despite her best efforts, the number of students in her class remained low. Three years passed and there was no change. She even contemplated changing career, but it was not easy giving up something she loved and was passionate about.

Aarti shared her problems with one of her friends, Sangeeta who listened to her patiently. She recommended Aarti to seek advice from her son, who was an expert in *MahaVastu*™. It was a

Saturday evening and Aarti called him up immediately. He agreed to come over on the following Monday.

On Monday afternoon, Aarti was waiting eagerly for the *MahaVastu*™ expert. He entered her house and went around, observing and making notes. He then devised an accurate floor plan and calculated the direction her house was facing. Later, he worked as per the four step *MahaVastu*™ method.

MahaVastu™ *Observations*

Directions and Rooms

The location of the entrance was in the S3 zone, which was fine and not causing any issues. The West (W) and the West-South-West (WSW) zones had weak zonal strength, due to which Aarti was not getting the expected gains, despite all her efforts.

Elements

A big blue coloured cooler was lying unused in the South (S) zone of the house. The kitchen was in the South-East (SE) zone, and a red-coloured fridge was placed along the Eastern wall.

Objects

There was a lot of clutter in the North Zone of the house (old newspapers, carry bags and empty sweet boxes were dumped there).

Evaluations

The *MahaVastu*™ expert evaluated that the West (W) and the West South West (WSW) zones of Aarti's house were weak. The blue cooler lying idle in the South (S) zone was also the reason why her coaching centre was not getting the rightful recognition. The clutter in the North zone was hindering receipt of money and hence stopping new students from joining Aarti's classes in spite best efforts.

Remedies

Once the *MahaVastu*™ expert was fully convinced that the problems and their symptoms matched hundred per cent, he outlined the solutions. He was delighted to use his knowledge to help others, since doing so gave him clarity. He suggested the following remedies:

- Strengthen the weak West (W) zone by using the 'Amplifier Technique'.
- Use 'Space Programming Technique' to treat the weak West-South-West (WSW) zone; hang a picture of books in this zone.
- Shift the blue-coloured cooler from the South to the North-North-West (NNW) zone of the house. Also, move the red-fridge in the kitchen to the South-South-East (SSE) zone.
- Lastly, he advised clearing all the clutter from North (N) Zone and placing a green plant in that area.

Results

Aarti followed all the recommendations of the *MahaVastu*™ expert religiously. After six weeks, Aarti came to Sangeeta's house to thank her and her son, who had changed her life. Aarti had benefited greatly and said, "in the last 15-days, the students' strength has increased from 15 to 55. Now, I am so busy that I need to start more classes. I have also increased the tuition fee which students are paying happily. I have got success beyond my expectations." While sharing her magical results, her eyes were moist with gratitude. After a year, Aarti had to shift to a bigger place to accommodate her large numbers of students. Associate teachers joined her classes as well. Today, Aarti is well known for the excellent results her students deliver. She later enrolled herself into the '*MahaVastu*™ learning course' so that she could design her new coaching centre herself.

❀

Enjoying Better Health

Dinesh was suffering from asthma and he used an inhaler quite often. Apart from this, his general immunity was growing weaker day-by-day. His health was deteriorating so much that he remained hospitalised frequently. He was taking a lot of medication, but the treatment was not helping him much. He changed doctors and tried alternate systems of therapy like Ayurveda, Homeopathy and Naturopathy. Yet, all the efforts failed to help.

One of the doctors who saw Dinesh happened to be a firm believer in *MahaVastu*™. He recommended Dinesh to get his home checked by a *MahaVastu*™ expert. Initially, Dinesh was reluctant since he feared that *Vastu* advisors recommend demolitions and alterations in the building. The very thought of renovations reminded him of dust and he felt scared of the allergy he had with it. However, when his doctor shared his personal experiences about the application of *MahaVastu*™ remedies in his home as well as clinic, Dinesh was convinced.

A *MahaVastu*™ expert visited Dinesh's home. The expert analysed the house-plan using the four-step method. He looked at the entrance, the rooms, the elements and the objects present in the space to draw an evaluation and recommend changes.

MahaVastu™ *Observations*

Directions and Rooms

- The entrance of the building was located at S7.

- The bedroom was located in North-East (NE) zone, (zone of water).
- The South-East (SE) and the South-South-East (SSE) zones possessed poor zonal strengths as per the *MahaVastu*™ bar chart analysis.

Elements

No elemental imbalance was found.

Objects

A washing machine was lying in the North-North-East (NNE) zone. This was responsible for reducing body's resistance in combating the asthma problem.

Evaluations

The *MahaVastu*™ expert evaluated that the building's entrance in S7 was the reason for loss of vitality in Dinesh. The location of Dinesh's bedroom in North East (NE) zone was the reason for increasing Kapha. Also the South-East (SE) and the South-South-East (SSE) zones had poor zonal strengths and the washing machine in the North-North-East (NNE) zone was reducing Dinesh's body resistance against disease.

Remedies

The first and the foremost rule of *MahaVastu*™ is that 'all the problematic symptoms should match hundred per cent with the four steps of *MahaVastu*™; only then should you suggest solutions.' Since the symptoms matched hundred per cent, the *MahaVastu*™ expert was confident of the successful results and suggested the following recommendations:

- He suggested that the negative effects of the entrance location be rectified by using the right colour in the house (to stop the loss of vitality).

- He suggested relocating the bedroom to the South-South-East (SSE) zone of the building as the zone of Fire would help increase Pitta and give strength to his body.
- He advised placing a red bulb in the South zone to improve the strength of that zone.
- He also suggested shifting the washing machine from the Health zone (North-North-East) to the terrace.

Results

Four weeks later, a new Dinesh emerged! His doctor called the *MahaVastu*™ expert and gave the good news that the medicines were now helping. Three months later, Dinesh was fit enough to lead a regular life and follow a good routine. He was so impressed with the *MahaVastu*™ expert that he not only recommended lots of clients, but also enrolled his two daughter-in-laws into MIRA (*MahaVastu*™ Institute for Research in Architecture) to learn this science.

✻

Experience Marital Bliss

Lokesh was a government officer who had been working for 15 years in the same field. He was appreciated by his superiors and colleagues for his intelligence and smooth working skills, and also enjoyed a happy personal life with his beautiful wife and two kids. After earning good money over a couple of years, Lokesh bought a house for his family. He had just spent about a year in the new house and he started feeling, things were not going quite well in his domestic life. Although everybody around him felt that he had a perfect life and nothing was going wrong, Lokesh started being disturbed and unhappy. In fact, his relationship with his wife turned sour, soon after they shifted in the new house. They exchanged heated arguments almost every day. The minute Lokesh reached home in the evening, his wife started complaining and yelling over trivial issues.

The trivial arguments kept accumulating over the next few months. This even impacted the kids who were scared and confused why their parents were fighting most of the time. This made Lokesh irritable and frustrated. As a reaction, he started going home as late as possible. He also took to drinking and smoking and avoided his wife as much as he could.

One day, Lokesh was sitting in the office after the work hours were over. His colleague, Mahesh asked him why he looked so pale and unhappy. Lokesh was so disturbed that he narrated the entire story. Fortunately, there was a *MahaVastu*™ seminar that was coming up in their city the next day itself. Mahesh took along Lokesh to that seminar.

During the seminar, Lokesh learnt about the scientific and logical aspects of *MahaVastu*™. He also listened to the live case studies by various *MahaVastu*™ experts and how they got the desired results by applying simple and easy techniques.

Lokesh decided to meet a *MahaVastu*™ expert and seek advice regarding his problem. He showed his house plan to the expert and discussed all his problems with ease. He narrated the innumerable instances when they had fought for no rational reason. The *MahaVastu*™ expert studied Lokesh's house (to-scale) and then visited the house. He applied the four steps method again, i.e., entrance, rooms, elements and objects, to draw and evaluate the *Vastu* situation and recommend changes.

MahaVastu™ *Observations*

Directions and Rooms

- The house's main entrance door was in E4. This ensured good financial conditions, especially through association with the government.
- Lokesh's bedroom was in the SSW, SW and WSW zones and the bed was placed in SW zone.

Elements

No elemental imbalance was found there.

Objects

The *MahaVastu*™ expert was shocked to see the couple's marriage photograph in the 'zone of disposal' and realised the root cause of why their relationship was disposing off.

Evaluations

The *MahaVastu*™ expert immediately recalled one of the lectures of Vastushastri Khushdeep Bansal, which said, "Sleeping in South-West zone gradually increases the couple's expectations from each other." This is what was being experienced by Lokesh and his wife. He also realised that the couple's marriage-photograph in the 'Zone of Disposal' was the root cause of ruining their relationship.

Remedies

The *MahaVastu*™ expert now suggested Lokesh and his wife a few changes in their house. The expert assured that the couple would experience a remarkable change in their relationship if they moved their bed a little to the WSW zone.

He suggested removing their marriage photograph from the 'zone of Disposal' and keeping it in the SW zone, the 'zone of relationships and bonding'.

Results

Lokesh followed *MahaVastu*™ expert's advice and incorporated the remedies. Twenty three days later, Lokesh and his wife came to see the *MahaVastu*™ expert.

"We were just passing by and thought of dropping in to see you," said Lokesh, "I have taken a week off and tomorrow we are leaving for Manali."

The *MahaVastu*™ expert could easily see the change in their relationship and he was wondering whether Lokesh's wife had started understanding him or Lokesh had stopped expecting too much from her! However, he was glad that his work was done!

❈

More Order and Sales

Kanchan was a multi-talented girl. She was good at arts and crafts and from a very young age, enjoyed mirror painting, sculpture and pottery. She loved presenting her work to friends and relatives. Even after getting married, she continued her hobby. Her husband, who was a businessman, suggested developing it into a full-fledged business. Kanchan was excited about it, and they made the necessary arrangements.

She worked very hard, and got several pieces ready for sale. Her husband gave her a room in the house, where she could keep the finished art pieces. The sales were good in the initial days and Kanchan was able to deliver the orders on time. However, soon, she started losing clients. When her regular customers did not turn up, Kanchan got worrying.

Mrs. Ahuja, a regular customer, ordered fifty pieces of hand-painted clay pots for Diwali gifts. But for some reason, she rejected the order after seeing the finished pieces. Kanchan was devastated.

Her assistant suggested that Kanchan should meet her friend — a *MahaVastu*™ expert. After some thought, Kanchan met the expert and shared her house plan and the issues with it.

The expert asked if she had shifted something red in colour to a room in the North side of the house, to make space. After some thought, Kanchan said that she had shifted a spare gas cylinder in the Northern room.

The expert told Kanchan not to worry and asked if she could visit her house and see the architectural plan. Once she was at the house, the expert applied the four steps, namely, entrance, rooms, elements and objects, and observed the following:

MahaVastu™ *Observations*

Directions and Rooms
- The main entrance door of the house was in the E4 zone. This ensured good financial conditions.
- Kanchan was using a room in the SSW Zone as a store.

Elements
- The kitchen was in the SE zone and did not cause any problems.
- The red gas cylinder in the Northern room caused an elemental imbalance.

Objects

Finished goods for sale were lying in the store in SSW zone. This was the reason that her total material was being rejected and dumped.

Evaluations

The *MahaVastu*™ expert evaluated that the material placed in the zone of disposal was the root cause of the problem.

Remedies

The *MahaVastu*™ expert suggested a few changes that Kanchan had to make in her house. She was sure that with the following remedies, Kanchan's business would pick up immediately:

- The gas cylinder should be shifted to its previous place in the back balcony of the kitchen in the SE zone, the zone of fire.
- Remove all the material for sale from the SSW room.
- Use Space Enlightening Technique of *MahaVastu*™ in the North Zone.

Results

As per the *MahaVastu*™ expert's suggestion, Kanchan and her husband reversed the activity in the N and SSW rooms within four days. After nine days, Kanchan called the *MahaVastu*™ expert and told her that she got two bulk orders from her clients. She thanked her for her guidance.

❁

Improve Studies

Mr. V.P. Mittal was facing a peculiar situation. After a long wait, he had managed to purchase his own house — a duplex builder-floor in a reputed posh locality of the capital city. The whole family was happy for their achievement.

Unfortunately, that happiness did not last long. Soon, Mrs. Mittal came to know from her new neighbours, that her house had been lying vacant since a long time. She was shocked to hear that it was considered an inauspicious or jinxed property. Initially, when she narrated all this to Mr. Mittal, he dismissed her notions and advised her to ignore all such nonsense. However, as time went by, unpleasant changes in their life made them believe that there was something wrong in that house.

Mr. Mittal's family was small with his wife, and two kids. They had a boy, 14, studying in the ninth standard, and a girl, 11. Within a year of shifting to this house, their son, who used to be a top-scoring student, started becoming careless in his studies. He lost interest in being the best. He scored only 53% in the examinations while none of his friends scored less than 80.

Mr Mittal approached a *MahaVastu*™ expert, as per the strong recommendations of his brother-in-law.

"Please tell me your problems in detail." asked the *MahaVastu*™ expert. Mr. Mittal said, "My son was reasonably good in his studies earlier, but since the past few months, he wastes his time surfing the Internet, looking at content which is unsuitable for a child of his age. If we say something to him, he becomes aggressive. I feel helpless." He continued, "These days I am facing instability in my business too. My landlord has asked me to vacate the space which I had been using for the past twenty years. My son cannot even bank upon my personal business. If he does not concentrate on his studies now, what he would do with his life? After all, he is the one who has to support us in the future. These issues keep haunting me and to tell you the truth, this is the reason why I have become quite short-tempered. In the previous house we used to sit together and laugh and enjoy, but ever since we shifted to this house, frustrations, anger and temper tantrums have marred our laughter and happiness. My mind is always occupied with these issues. I don't know what to do. Do you think all this is due to some negativity present in our building?" The expert listened to them attentively and said, "Don't worry, everything will be soon alright."

After this, he observed their house and applied the four steps of *MahaVastu*™, entrance, rooms, elements and objects on their house plan, to draw an evaluation and recommend changes.

MahaVastu™ *Observations*

Directions and Rooms
- The Entrance was located in E6.
- The son's bedroom was located in NNW Zone.
- Mr. and Mrs. Mittal's bedroom was located in WSW Zone.
- SE and ESE Zones of the house were extended.

Elements
- The Kitchen was located in the NE Zone creating an elemental imbalance.
- Mr. and Mrs. Mittal's bedroom was painted in green colour. This disturbed their son's focus on studies and also affected the stability of their business.

Objects
A computer was placed in NNW Zone in the son's bedroom. This was acting as a tool for getting sensual pleasures.

Evaluations

The expert realised that the symptoms matched hundred per cent with the problems. The location of the Entrance in E6 meant that a person cannot keep his words. The location of their son's bedroom and computer in the zone of sex, made him more inclined to surf such stuff on Internet. The extended SE and ESE zones of the house were increasing aggression and worries. The location of the kitchen was also causing heated arguments, blurred vision, and confusions thus affecting his business negatively. The green paint in Mr. Mittal's bedroom was causing his son's lack of interest in his studies.

Remedies

After a detail observation, he recommended the following solutions: The entrance should be painted with a yellow colour strip to make the family more committed.

- Mr. and Mrs. Mittal's bedroom was interchanged with their son's bedroom, so that the son would sleep in the WSW or the zone of education.
- The colour of the WSW room was changed to white.
- The walls of the SE Zone were painted yellow.
- The *Tattva-Shuddhi* and amplifier techniques of *MahaVastu*™ were used in the kitchen, to improve clarity of mind and concentration.
- The books and the computer were shifted to WSW Zone.
- The changes revived their son's interest towards studies. He started using the computer for educational purposes.

Results

"Just make these changes, and tell me how you feel," said the expert before leaving.

After four months, Mr. Mittal approached him again. "We are going to shift our office to a new place. I need your assistance to set *MahaVastu*™ compliance in it, so that everything goes well."

"Sure, how is your son doing now?" asked the expert. "He is doing well. He scored 86% in his final examinations. He speaks properly and does not waste time on the computer. I don't worry like before. I just want to establish my business in the new location," replied Mr. Mittal.

"Don't worry, that will also happen," said the expert.

❊

Let Money Flow

Mohit and his wife, Priya were a happy couple who lived in Gurgaon. Mohit worked in Noida in an export house, as a senior marketing manager. He had worked hard to move to a senior position. His boss and subordinates loved to work with him. His boss especially considered him an asset to the company.

Mohit spent a lot of time travelling from Gurgaon to Noida every day. He wanted to save time and hence, decided to shift his residence to Noida. Mohit and Priya found a nice apartment to live in and they happily shifted there.

Things went well for the first four months. Then, Mohit noticed that he was disagreeing with his bosses. Soon, Mohit started getting into heated arguments at work over small issues. His boss could not believe that Mohit was acting this way. Ultimately, Mohit lost his job. However, he did not lose heart and remained confident of his potential. He was sure of finding another job soon. He started applying at various companies in and around Delhi. Though he did all the interviews well, not a single offer materialised from anywhere.

He then started applying for jobs outside the country. Eight months had passed and Mohit hadn't yet found work. He and his wife Priya were extremely worried now. Their financial condition was also not very good.

One day, Priya met her old friend who was a *MahaVastu*™ expert. She explained how things had turned out for Mohit in the past few months. The expert asked Priya if there was an inverter in the North of the house. Priya asked her to visit the home.

The *MahaVastu*™ expert marked the layout of the furniture on the plan. She then applied the four steps method that is, entrance, rooms, elements and objects, to draw an evaluation and recommend changes.

MahaVastu™ *Observations*

Directions and Rooms
- The entrance to the house was lying in N2. This was not an ausoicious entrance as it Invited enmity and jealousy and blocked prosperity.
- One half of the drawing room and another half of the entrance lobby were lying in the N Zone.

Elements
Kitchen was in the NE zone causing an elemental imbalance.

Objects
An inverter was kept in the drawing room in N zone.

Evaluations

After analysing the house completely, the *MahaVastu*™ expert evaluated the problem in Mohit's house. She found that the entrance of the house was not at all good. It caused enmity and jealousy. This had caused Mohit arguments at work. Kitchen, the fire element was placed in the *Puja* activity zone. This caused elemental imbalance leading to heated arguments. The inverter placed in the N zone created an emergency-like situation in Mohit's career.

Remedies

She suggested some changes which would help Mohit regain lost opportunities. She suggested the following remedies:

- Use the Space Surgery Technique of *MahaVastu*™ to manage the bad effects of the entrance.
- Shift the gas stove from NE to ENE zone with the help of the *Tattva-Shuddhi* technique.
- A zero-watt red bulb in the SE Zone, which lit up part of the balcony and the toilet, would speed up the process.
- Inverter was to be shifted from the entrance using Activity Relocation technique.
- A green-scene was put up in the drawing room.
  Mohit and Priya made the suggested changes within three days.

Results

In a week, Priya called the *MahaVastu*™ expert and told her that Mohit had got a great offer from a multinational company and he was joining the firm soon. Priya was happy and thanked her from the heart.

❖

Financial Stability

Mr. Puneet, a Senior Sales Manager in a multinational company in Gurgaon from six years never faced any problems at his workplace and enjoyed healthy relations with his colleagues and bosses. His wife Neha, a talented Software Programmer worked in an IT firm and she too was doing well. Both of them were happy together and life was progressing smoothly until they had a baby. Soon after Neha gave birth to a baby boy, she decided to give up her job to take care of the child.

Life became a difficult for the new parents, and within some time, Puneet started facing difficulties at his workplace. Problems kept piling up, one after the other. His boss started complaining about the output, and sometimes, he would have issues with the customers. This continued for a few months.

Finally, Puneet got fed up and quit his job. He thought that he would easily find a better option in a good company, since his work-profile and experience in the field of sales was impressive. However, five months passed by and he did not receive any good offers. The couple started facing financial problems and this affected their peace and personal relationship too. Both of them were worried since they had to take care of their baby too. Neha regretted her decision of quitting her job.

At last, Puneet contacted a *MahaVastu*™ expert whom he knew through a common friend. Both Puneet and Neha met her and explained the problems they were facing.

The *MahaVastu*™ expert asked them whether they had done anything to the Northern area of their house. Puneet admitted that they had re-painted the entire house just before the birth of their son. This information was enough for the expert to gauge the problem. She asked them, if they had used pink paint in their house. Puneet and Neha were surprised that she had guessed the colour they had used. The *MahaVastu*™ expert reassuringly asked them to get the house-plan draft to scale.

After a week, she visited Puneet's house. She took the directions and marked the furniture layout and colours in the house plan. She then applied the four steps of *MahaVastu*™, that is entrance, rooms, elements and objects, to draw an evaluation and recommend changes.

MahaVastu™ *Observations*

Directions and Rooms

- The main entrance door of the house was in the S3 zone, not causing any problems.
- The bedroom was in the North zone.
- The toilet was in the South zone.

Elements

- The bedroom being painted in pink created a disturbance in the careers.
- Blue coloured tiles in the toilet led to financial crunch and losses.

Objects

A painting depicting scenery with a prominent red house was hung in the bedroom.

Evaluations

The *MahaVastu*™ expert realised the root cause of the problem was elemental-imbalance arising out of the wrong usage of colours.

Remedies

After a detail observation, she recommended the following solutions.

- Repaint the house and remove the pink colour from the North zone.
- Put green-colored scenery on the Northern wall.

- A zero watt red bulb in was placed the Southern toilet, which would remain on for 24 hours.
- She asked them to display their qualification certificates in their bedroom.

Results

As Neha and Puneet were jobless and had time, they immediately did all the remedial work in their house within a period of five days.

Within two weeks of the remedial work, Puneet got a great offer from a reputed multinational company through one of his friends. Neha too applied for freelance projects and started working. Both of them were happily surprised to see things changing. They were overwhelmed with the positive changes that occurred within 15 days of applying *MahaVastu*™ remedies and also that their problems had disappeared in a flash.

❄

Health and Healing Energy

Mr. Dhar, a simple man was the head of his family. He had just retired from the government service with a good pension. Throughout his life, he had worked hard for securing a comfortable future for his wife and two sons. It was with this view, that he built a new house for them. Post retirement, Mr. Dhar and family shifted from their government quarter to the new home. Within six years of shifting into this new house, Mr. Dhar started facing health problems. His health deteriorated and he kept losing weight. He tried different treatments — Allopathic, Ayurvedic and Homeopathic, but the illness persisted. From a healthy 84 kgs, he had reduced to mere

69 kgs. Due to his declining health and increasing boredom, he started losing interest in life and started sinking into depression.

His family tried their level best to find solutions, but Mr. Dhar refused any further treatment. His wife, Mrs. Dhar then approached a friend who knew a *MahaVastu*™ expert. She explained the entire situation to the expert.

The *MahaVastu*™ expert visited Mrs. Dhar's house. She studied the house plan and applied the four steps of *MahaVastu*™ — entrance, rooms, elements and objects, to draw an evaluation and recommend changes.

MahaVastu™ *Observations*

Directions and Rooms

- Location of the entrance was alright and not causing any problems.
- The SSW Zone in their house was very large.
- Mr. and Mrs. Dhar's bedroom was in the same Zone (SSW) for the last six years.

Elements

No Elemental imbalance was found there

Objects

Placement of objects too was fine and not causing any problems.

Evaluations

The *MahaVastu*™ expert realised that the root cause of the problems was the vast SSW Zone containing the master bedroom. Mr. Dhar's health deterioration was because of this.

Remedies

After a detail observation, the expert recommended shifting the bedroom to N-NE and NE zones.

Results

Mrs. Dhar immediately changed their bedroom location though it took her some time convincing her husband. Sometime later, Mr. Dhar agreed consulting a different doctor for his medical problems. This time the diagnosis was clear — he had intestinal infection. He received proper treatment and was cured within six months. He regained his jest for life! In fact Mr. Dhar got an invitation to join a private company as a consultant, which made good use of his expertise in government service. His family couldn't be happier and Mrs. Dhar called her friend to thank her for enlightening her with *MahaVastu*™.

❂

Clarity of Mind

Harminder Singh, a resident of Khanna, Punjab, inherited a thriving milk business from his great-grandfathers. Their business enjoyed a clean reputation because of the quality that had been their hallmark over the past many years. Harminder worked hard and raised the standard of his business through dutiful customer service and newer methods of quality control. After some time, he tried diversifying the business into milk products as well. He added a range of milk products to their catalogue, ranging from cottage cheese, butter, buttermilk, *ghee* (clarified butter) to ice-creams. However, the expected revenues from this diversification did not meet Harminder's expectations. He had invested a lot of money in expanding the business and adding cattle stock.

Over this time, Harminder's personal life too went through rough weather. His mother was diagnosed with cancer and she remained bed-ridden. As a result, Harminder developed stress-related issues like high blood-pressure and insomnia. His work efficiency and overall business were suffering badly. The age-long reputation of his family business was gradually going to ruins — Harminder could only watch silently and get frustrated.

One day, when Harminder took his mother for a routine check up to the city hospital, he met a distant relative who already knew about the business-related issues he was facing. Since the communities across Punjab cities and villages are very close-knit, people usually become aware of each others' problems quick. This in fact furthered Harminder's woes since he hated people blaming him for tarnishing the family's reputation. His cousin, in a passing reference, mentioned about a *MahaVastu*™ expert in Ludhiana.

Harminder saw a ray of hope and wasted no time in contacting him. He too somewhere felt, that the recent constructions in his home were causing a negative impact on his life — especially, because the problems he was facing had no particular or rational cause.

The *MahaVastu*™ expert visited Harminder's house and interacted with his mother. Harminder poured out his experiences to the expert who listened very attentively. He then expressed the desire to observe the house. He applied four steps of *MahaVastu*™, entrance, rooms, elements and objects, on their house plan.

MahaVastu™ *Observations*

Directions and Rooms
- Entrance: W4-W5. This entrance, as analysed by the expert, made Harminder too much of a perfectionist and inclined towards hasty and incorrect decisions.
- The North-East zone of the house was at a raised height, being used for keeping the cattle.
- The bedroom was located in the South-West, but had a mirror hanging there.

Elements
A mirror hung on the South wall was bringing ill-repute.

Objects
The East was totally cluttered with the buffalo fodder dumped in it.

Evaluations
The expert evaluated that the imbalance of Earth and Water elements gave way to an imbalance in Harminder's life. This affected his decision-making abilities and blocked his mind from making a clear picture of life.

Remedies
Since it was an old house, a haveli, not many construction-related remedies were suggested. The *MahaVastu*™ expert customised an easy-to-follow plan for the client.

Here are some of the measures:
- The entrance of the house was painted white.
- Since the client's mother occupied the bedroom in South-South West (SSW) direction, a yellow pot was placed there to bring health-related benefits.

- The mirror in the South was covered to control elemental imbalance.
- *Khurli,* the place for keeping fodder, was moved from the North-East zone.
- Most importantly, the clutter in the East zone was cleaned up, for improving growth and social connectivity in the client's life.

Results

Harminder's belief in *MahaVastu*™ was genuine and his efforts sincere. He followed the *MahaVastu*™ expert's advice and incorporated the remedies. Within just two months, he regained his confidence and self-worth. His worrisome attitude towards business was gradually replaced by a clear thought process. He analysed all his business propositions, both the old milk production unit and the new milk-products unit. With a planned approach and a well-thought-out business strategy, he was able to revive his family's business. Harminder's mother, too felt desirable changes in terms of renewed energy in the house.

Like Harminder, there are many people out there who believe in hard work, dedication and honesty. However, an imbalance in the five essential elements prevents them from reaching the heights they truly deserve. *MahaVastu*™ has remedies for all such people out there.

It is now clear that whatever be the type of problem in your life, its solution is possible. All you need is seeing how the energies in your house are defining situations in your life. Learning that methodology will help you know the root causes of your problems and your subconscious mind will proceed for their solutions instead of just worrying about them.

As we have mentioned before, your life and the situations you face are governed by your subconscious mind only, which in turn, is controlled by your immediate physical surroundings (your Home, Office etc).

The four aspects of your house, namely Location of Entrance; Location of Rooms; Presence of Five Elements; and, Location of Objects, together, decide which emotions and ideas are being transplanted in your subconscious mind. Whatever emotions and impressions you carry in your subconscious mind; it considers them as your desires and starts coordinating with natural earth energies for their manifestation. As a result, you start behaving in such manner, coming across such people, and receiving such situations which take you towards that result (desired or undesired). So, your subconscious mind is like a computer chip which can be programmed for desired manifestations.

❀

5. *MahaVastu*™ for Everyday Life

Mentioned below are some of the tested and effective *MahaVastu*™ Tips for your daily life. All these are logically based on the 4-Step Method, repeatedly applied by trained *MahaVastu*™ Experts. These will not only help you program your space for positive results but also, deprogram the existing negative space arrangements to pave the way for your growth, success, love and happiness.

- No new ideas will come to you, if your building has blocked zone of clarity and mind. Clean the NE zone of red, orange, and dark yellow colours to improve its positive effects and conceive new ideas.

- Keeping a bunch of fresh flowers in a green vase in the zone of recreation and fun will bring more fun and happiness in your life.

- To get new growth opportunities in your job, keep a 'money plant' in the zone of money and opportunities in your house.

- Medicines should be kept in the zone of health and immunity. This increases their effectiveness.

- Kitchen in East of Southeast zone increases anxiety in general for every member of the family, leading to clashes and dispute. Prolonged use of this kitchen also leads to health problems like blood pressure and diabetes.

- Red flowers kept in the Southeast zone in your house add warmth in your relationships.

- Avoid placing your cupboard in the zone of expenditure and wastage so as to control wasteful expenditure and get better results of your efforts.

- A family photograph placed in the zone of relationship and skills always strengthens love and bonding among the family members.

- Study table of children should be placed in the zone of education. This will draw their natural inclination towards studies and help them secure better grades.

- Avoid storing useless and junk articles in the zone of gains, as it will adversely affect your savings and overall gains in life.

- Sleeping in the zone of depression over the years, leads to development of severe ailments like thyroid.

- A store of useful articles placed in the North-West zone helps you get the support of people in the hour of need.

- To ensure love and warm relations with your spouse, keep a statue of pair of white horses in the zone of sex and attraction.

- Sprinkle "non-iodized sea-salt" all over the floor and then sweep it away to re-energise your space. Remember not to cross-over it.

- To make best use of computers by children at home, place them along the Western wall.

- To get rid of negative thoughts, clean the Northeast zone of clutter and other waste articles in your house.

GLOSSARY

Aakash
Space; In *Mahavastu*™ by *Aakash* we mean Space inside a building and more precisely, the Space within an atom which is a conscious field that binds electrons, protons and neutrons within the atom. So, in *Mahavastu*™, Space does not mean an empty space but a conscious field in any given space.

Abhyaas
Practice

Acharya
A master who shows the way and teaches you awareness of a subject

Agneya Koan
Zone of the Fire Element

Agni
Fire; the very driving force of each and every process of life

Anandmaya Kosha
The perfect state of Existence; the supreme, Blissful state of consciousness

Annamaya Kosha
Material manifested world; physical body; the lower most state of consciousness

Ashoka
A famous King of Maurya Dynasty

Atma / Atman
Soul; the conscious self; the central axis of space inside the human body

Aum
The primitive sound of Space which is heard at deeper levels of meditation, where human

	awareness transits from the alpha to the theta levels of brain wave frequencies
Ayurveda	'*Aayu*' means 'Life' + '*Veda*' means 'Knowledge'; Indian medicinal knowledge for health and wellbeing
Chakras	Energy vortices inside the human body along the spinal chord
Chandra Nadi	Refer to '*Ida*'
Daaridrya	Poverty
Deepak	Earthen pot; traditional lamp filled with oil that is lit
Dev-Sthaan	Where any potential deity or the soul guide with whom you communicate with in a meditative state reside
Dhoop	Incense
Dosh	Defect
Durga Mata	The Goddess/Mother *Durga*
Dwarpal	Door-keeper
Garbhagriha	*Garbhagriha* is a Sanskrit word meaning the 'interior of the sanctum sanctorum'; the innermost sanctum of a Hindu temple where the *murti* (idol or icon) of the primary deity of the temple resides. Literally the word means 'womb chamber' derived from the Sanskrit word *garbha* for 'womb' and

griha for 'house'. Generally, the *garbhagriha* is a windowless and sparsely lit chamber, intentionally created to focus the devotee's mind on the tangible form of the Divine within it.

Guna-Dharma	Attributes
Gurukul	A place, usually set outside the city, where students lived with their teachers and gained knowledge directly from the Master, primarily by means of experiences.
Hanuman	Supreme devotee of Lord Rama; worshipped as a symbol of strength and the reliever from problems
Ida	Breath flowing through the left nostril; has qualities of the Moon; represents feminine energy
Ishaan	North-East (NE) Zone; Zone of Water
Jal	Water; everything that floats and nurtures growth comes under the domain of the Water element.
Jagat	*Samsara*; the visible world
Kosha	Layer; sheet
Kundalini	A dormant energy present in every human being, which is awakened through *Yogic, Tantrik* practices or, sometimes it awakens by itself in intense emotional states.
Lord Ganesha	A Hindu deity considered most auspicious, worshipped at the commencement of any work

	so as to ensure its completion sans hurdles and problems.
Maha *Vastu*	'*Maha*' means 'Great' and '*Vastu*' (see *Vastu*)
Mandap	Any structure erected that is meant for ritual purposes
Manomaya Kosha	Mental body; Mind body; out of 'Five Layers of Existence', this is the central layer which connects the Energy body and Insight/ Intuitive body.
Nandi Bull	Nandi is the bull which Lord Shiva rides and is Shiva's gatekeeper and principal *gana* (attendant) in Hindu mythology.
Panchkosha	'Five Layers of Existence'
Panchtattva	Five elements of nature
Param Shiv	Supreme consciousness; Shiva *tattva* is the absolute phenomenon responsible for creation
Parvati	A Hindu Goddess; wife of Lord Shiva and Mother of Lord Ganesha
Pingala	Breath flowing through the right nostril; has qualities of the Sun; represents masculine energy.
Poorva Abhas	Premonition; intuition
Prana	Life-force; Consciousness
Prani	Living being
Pranmaya Kosha	Energy body; out of five layers of Existence, this is

the layer just below the conscious state; it pertains to alpha level of brain wave frequencies.

Prasad	Palace
Prithvi	Earth; most revered of the five elements providing stability in life
Puja	To worship
Pujaniya	Worthy of being Worshipped
Rati	Goddess of sex in Hindu mythology
Rodhan	Weeping, crying
Samkhya Yoga Darshan	Indian metaphysics
Sarvapratham	First of all
Shakti Tattva	The creative force
Shastra	The word is generally used as a suffix in the context of technical or specialised knowledge in a defined area of practice.
Shlokas	The Sanskrit term *shloka* specifically denotes a metered and, often, rhymed poetic verse or phrase.
Shudhi	The act of cleaning
Sthoola	The act of cleaning
Sukhinah	Happy and prosperous
Surya Dev	Sun God
Surya Nadi	Refer *Pingala*

Sutras	Formulae
Swaroopen Awasthanam	Establishing in one's own self
Swastika	Ancient Hindu symbol
Taittiriya Upanishad	The *Taittriya Upanishad* is one of the older, 'primary' Upanishads commented upon by Shankara. It is associated with the *Taittiriya* School of the Black Yajurveda. It reveals details of the creation of the universe.
Tattva	Element
Tridosha	*Tri* means 'three' and *Dosha* means 'defect'; *Vaat, Pitta, Kapha* – the three fundamental characteristics naturally present inside a human body, as described in *Ayurveda*, that control the metabolism of the body.
Triguna	*Tri* means 'three' and *Guna* means 'attribute'; *Sattva, Rajas, Tamas* –the three basic attributes, as described in Yoga, governing a person on the Mind-Body level (*Manomaya Kosha*), namely, the mental state, thoughts, intentions and attitude.
Vastu	Derived from the word *vas-niwase*, meaning 'habitable place'
Vayavya Koan	Zone of Air
Vayu	Air; one of the five elements, responsible for growth and connectivity with the outer world

Vedanta	Vedic wisdom; *Veda* means 'knowledge' and *Anta* is the 'essence', 'core', or 'inside'; thus, Vedanta is the essence of the *Vedas*. Vedanta is a spiritual tradition explained in the Upanishads for being concerned with self-realisation by which one understands the ultimate nature of reality (*Brahman*) and learns that the believer's goal is to transcend the limitations of self-identity and realise one's unity with *Brahman*.
Vidya	Knowledge
Vigyanmaya Kosha	Intuitive body; the layer of consciousness, which is responsible for intuition and healing powers
Vishwakarma Prakash	An ancient book containing the tenets of *Vastu Shastra*
Yaksharaj Kuber	*Yaksha* is the name of a broad class of nature-spirits, usually benevolent, who are caretakers of the natural treasures hidden in the Earth and tree roots. *Kuber* is the King of *Yakshas* and the Lord of wealth in Hindu mythology. He is the guardian of the North (N) Zone. Brahma, the Creator, gave him immortality and made him the God of wealth and the guardian of all the treasures of the Earth, the *Nidhi*.
Yantras	*Yantras* are instruments, symbolic representations, or objects supposed to relieve one from the negative effects or adverse situations in life.

Yoga

Yoga refers to the traditional physical and mental disciplines originating in India; to the goal achieved by those disciplines; and to one of the six orthodox (*āstika*) schools of Hindu philosophy. The Sanskrit word 'Yoga' has many meanings, and is derived from the Sanskrit root *yuj*, meaning 'to control', 'to yoke' or 'to unite'.

EARTH'S BIGGEST BOOK ON VASTUSHASTRA

MahaVastu™ Handbook (English)

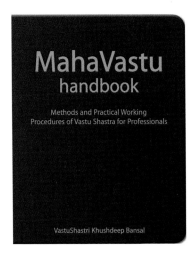

Selfhelp / Vastu
LeatherBack
236mm x 188mm (Portrait)
1,248 pages
ISBN 978-93-81570-10-4
₹ 1,25,000
US $ 7,295.95
UK £ 4,795.95

Earth's biggest book on Vastu Shastra, 'MahaVastu handbook' is practical, detailed, carries lot of new coloured diagrams with clear explanations on each and every aspect of Vastu Shastra. MahaVastu Handbook is an established standard reference for new Vastu enthusiasts and also, for Vastu professionals.

The book has hundreds of new successful MahaVastu case studies added to it. Now, whether it is planning and designing of a new building or, setting Vastu compliance in an interior decoration project or, solving any problem – you can do easily with 4-Step MahaVastu.

MahaVastu handbook lucidly explains how to:

- Work with the Earth energies and the energy fields of Vastu Purush Mandala.

- Read directions accurately and, recognise directional zones in a building.

- Correct harmful effects of wrong Entrance-locations with colours and metals.

- Use power of the Five-Elements for most effective and powerful solutions.

- Programme buildings with paintings and sculptures.

- Choose beneficial paintings.

- Apply the techniques of the Alchemy of Space.

- Manage cut portions in a building.

- Use the most powerful Sixteen Techniques to cure Vastu-dosha without resorting to demolitions in a building.

- Decide placement of different activities and objects in their right directions.

- Beneficial Colours in different directions.

With more than 600 images and 200 Vastu case studies you will get clear guidelines to successfully apply tested and effective Vastu remedies. And, get the best results in different domains of life like, better health, money, relationships, studies, security, bigger gains, exponential growth and many more.

READ MORE

MahaVastu™ (English, Hindi, Kindle)
(The No.1 India Today, March 2010 Bestseller)

Selfhelp / Vastu
PaperBack
178mm x 127mm (Portrait)
160 pages
ISBN 978-93-80069-37-1
₹ 295   US $ 22.95   UK £ 14.95

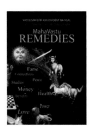

MahaVastu Remedies (English, Kindle)

Selfhelp / Vastu
PaperBack
178mm x 127mm (Portrait)
160 pages
ISBN 978-93-81570-21-0
₹ 295   US $ 22.95   UK £ 14.95

Vastu Shastra Today (Hindi)

Selfhelp / Vastu
PaperBack
159mm x 238mm (Portrait)
256 pages
ISBN 978-93-81570-23-4
₹ 395   US $ 29.95   UK £ 19.95

Alchemy of Growth (English, Hindi, Kindle)

Non-fiction / Alchemy
PaperBack
178mm x 127mm (Portrait)
176 pages
ISBN 978-93-81570-17-3
₹ 295   US $ 22.95   UK £ 14.95

Purpose of Life (English, Hindi, Kindle)

Non-fiction / Alchemy
PaperBack
178mm x 127mm (Portrait)
176 pages
ISBN 978-93-81570-16-6
₹ 295   US $ 22.95   UK £ 14.95

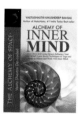

Alchemy of Inner Mind (English, Hindi, Kindle)

Non-fiction / Alchemy
PaperBack
178mm x 127mm (Portrait)
192 pages
ISBN 978-93-81570-18-0
₹ 295   US $ 22.95   UK £ 14.95

45 Powers of Alchemy (English, Hindi, Kindle)

Non-fiction / Alchemy
PaperBack
178mm x 127mm (Portrait)
272 pages
ISBN 978-93-81570-19-7
₹ 395   US $ 29.95   UK £ 19.95

Directions of Alchemy (English, Hindi, Kindle)

Non-fiction / Alchemy
PaperBack
178mm x 127mm (Portrait)
208 pages
ISBN 978-93-81570-20-3
₹ 395   US $ 29.95   UK £ 19.95

Dhyan (Hindi)

Selfhelp / Spirituality
PaperBack
178mm x 127mm (Portrait)
160 pages
ISBN 978-93-81570-12-8
₹ 295   US $ 22.95   UK £ 14.95

UNDER PUBLISHING

Karma Completion

Selfhelp / Spirituality
PaperBack
178mm x 127mm (Portrait)
160 pages
ISBN 978-93-81570-13-5
₹ 295   US $ 22.95   UK £ 14.95

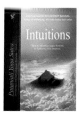

Intuitions

Selfhelp / Spirituality
PaperBack
178mm x 127mm (Portrait)
160 pages
ISBN 978-93-81570-14-2
₹ 295   US $ 22.95   UK £ 14.95

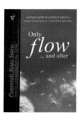

Only Flow

Selfhelp / Spirituality
PaperBack
178mm x 127mm (Portrait)
160 pages
ISBN 978-93-81570-15-9
₹ 295   US $ 22.95   UK £ 14.95

MahaVastu™ for Better Relationships (Kindle)

Selfhelp / Vastu
PaperBack
213mm x 140mm (Portrait)
268 pages
ISBN 978-93-81576-11-1
₹ 395   US $ 29.95   UK £ 19.95

Destiny

Selfhelp / Astrology
HardBack
236mm x 188mm (Portrait)
512 pages
ISBN 978-93-81570-09-8
₹ 12,500   US $ 795.95   UK £ 495.95

GET BEST VASTU ADVICE

Meet Your Vastu Expert

You will come to know the exact Vastu reasons for your problems in your meeting with well Qualified and Experienced MahaVastu Experts at Noida centre. People get amazed when MahaVastu Experts pin pointedly tell them what is placed where in their homes by just listening to their problems.

All you need is to come with floor Plan of your building and a list of your Problems or Goals that you are not successful in achieving. (Building Plans and List of Problems and Goals – these two things are most important for an effective and productive meeting.)

If you don't have building plan, it is better to draw it yourself for the first meeting with Maha Vastu Expert. Sometimes, as found in many cases, problems in life are not due to Vastu. But, Immature Vastu Advisors misguide and create confusions. According to MahaVastu system, 100% matching of symptoms Vs. reasons is required to get effective results and solutions to your problems. At MahaVastu Centre, after a quick & easy registration process, you will get a clear picture of whether you have any Vastu Problems or Not – Absolutely Free of Cost.

GET BEST VASTU ADVICE

Get Accurate Vastu Analysis

In your meeting, MahaVastu Expert concludes which area of your building needs more detailed Vastu survey and analysis to avoid demolitions and re-constructions. Only an accurate Vastu analysis done on a To-The-Scale plan of your building helps to make right decisions.

When found necessary, a detailed MahaVastu Survey of your building is done by a professional Vastu surveyor. It carries minute details about interior designs and objects in your home or/and office. In case of factory, it also contains all the important check-points (e.g., location and exact size of each machinery, storage of raw material and finished product, water tanks, boilers and furnaces, staff rooms and toilets, packing area, dispatch area, electric control panel, generators etc.).

A scientific and Accurate Vastu Analysis, based on MahaVastu survey report, is done by a senior MahaVastu Expert to find out the root cause of problems which you are facing or you will face in future due to your building.

4-Step MahaVastu Analysis entails detailed evaluation of more than 120 most important points which affect -

- In Home, all the aspects of your life, like, money, growth, gains, health, family harmony, child education, behaviour and many more.

- At Office, your important business aspects, namely, orders, sales, payment recovery, staff retention, banking support, departmental problems and relationship with your customers.

- In factory, sales, production, procurements, quality, sample approvals, departmental clearances, payment recovery, bank's support, and many other issues related with smooth working of an industry.

GET BEST VASTU ADVICE

Find Effective Vastu Solutions

Easy and Practical Solutions like Colour and metal strips inserting into floor to diminish negative effects of Entrance Doors and Toilets placed in wrong directions, coloured electric bulbs, paintings, art objects, stones, pyramids and many other tested and effective Vastu Remedies are suggested as per Accurate Vastu analysis. You can receive them in two ways – Without Site Visit and With Site Visit.

Astro Power : Use Power of Planets and Stars

Know which planets give you inner strengths to grow and succeed in life – in your Astro Benefit Report. After detailed analysis, Expert recommends you Fortune creating Gem Stones, beneficial Colours, your Soul Mantra and most Powerful Directions with related planets to attract Money, Health and Prosperity. It is prepared on the basis of a detailed analysis of your date of birth, time of birth and place of birth.

Numerology : Add Magic of Letters and Numbers

Now empower your name, signatures, brand and e-mail accounts with magical power of Lucky Numbers and Letters that Jews (world's richest community) believes in. In your Numero Power report, you get the same secret Kabbalah Numero code of Hebrew numbers used by eminent celebrities and luxury brands.

Contact:
MahaVastu Center, A 103, Sector 65, Noida - 201 301, Uttar Pradesh, India
Ph: 0120-4101990, 0120-4101991   Email: ask@mahavastu.com

GET LATEST INFORMATION ONLINE

Visit: www.mahavastu.com

MahaVastu™

Helps you to live with more happiness, love and prosperity

Benefits
- Attract More Money
- Get Big Order and Sales
- Maximize Industrial Production
- Get Best Product Quality
- Create New Opportunities
- Getting Fame & Recognition
- Create Financial Security
- Awaken Healing Energy at Home
- Strengthen Love & Relationships
- Improve Grades in Studies
- Stop Draining Money & Efforts
- Joy & Happiness

MahaVastu™

MahaVastu™ is a 4-Step Method to know the influence of your building (living or work place) on you and your life. These influences can be positive or negative and are, accordingly, responsible for your success or failure. The concept has been distilled from 10,000 successful research-based case studies done by VastuShastri....
Read more...

The Vastu Guru

Considered as the foremost Vastu expert in India, VastuShastri Khushdeep Bansal was born in Punjab in 1972. While studying Electronics Engineering in 1989, an observation struck his mind that certain....
Read more...

Learn Vastu

MahaVastu™ Program Offers two Courses
- MAHAVASTU™ COURSE
- ADVANCED MAHAVASTU™ COURSE

Book
MahaVastu Handbook
Read more
Buy Now

Aun kar
Foundation

" " We are committed to make this
valuable knowledge available to
each individual in the world, in
order to facilitate the uninterrupted
evolution of his or her being. So that
one can manifest the core purpose
of existence on Earth, as well as
make this world more joyous
and happier.